Capital Punishments

Crime and Prison Conditions in Victorian London

For Terry . . . . on the road to find out

INTRODUCTION

With over one million cases of domestic violence reported every year, an ever-increasing number of juvenile offenders and the prison service creaking at the seams, the main themes of 'Capital Punishments' are as relevant today as they were over a century ago.

In Victorian London, after murder, theft was considered the most serious offence, with cases of assault, when reported, resulting in fairly light sentences. Although we have now reversed this emphasis, both crimes are still all too common in today's society.

When reading about the crimes of violence in the opening chapters, one cannot help but notice the recurring scenario: alcohol, overcrowding, a poorly-educated population and grinding poverty.

In the second half of the book we follow those found guilty, of sometimes very minor offences, into gaol. With the end of transportation, a massive prison building programme had to be undertaken as penal servitude replaced earlier punishments. Different views as to how to reform the criminals were experimented with; these included a rule of total silence in some prisons, the wearing of masks, the treadwheel and enforced hard labour. Very few were reformed.

A true impression of the harsh conditions 'inside' is best gained from the prisoners who had to endure the strict regime and detailed extracts from their anonymous works have been quoted.

If you are interested in executions and conditions on the prison hulks these may be found in *'London . . . The Sinister Side'* details on page 88.

First published in 1992
Wicked Publications
222 Highbury Road, Bulwell, Nottingham NG6 9FE
Telephone: 0602 756828

Second Edition (revised) 1993

By the same Author

London . . . The Sinister Side

London Through the Keyhole

Wicked London

ISBN 1-870000-03

Typeset and printed in Great Britain by
J. W. Brown (Printers) Limited, Darwin Press,
77a Blackheath Road, Greenwich, London SE10 8PD.
Telephone: 081-691 1357

CONTENTS

ILLUSTRATION ACKNOWLEDGEMENTS

Many thanks are given to the following for permission to reproduce their pictures:

MARY EVANS PICTURE LIBRARY
13, 14, 16, 33, 35, 36, 42, 45, 47, 48, 49, 66, 67.

THE HULTON DEUTSCH COLLECTION
41, 43, 46, 63, 68, 71, 85, 87.

GREENWICH LIBRARY
5, 37.

G.L.C. LIBRARY
4, 6, 9, 21, 22, 23, 24, 27, 28, 30, 54.

THE ILLUSTRATED LONDON NEWS PICTURE LIBRARY
25, 76, 78, 82, 83.

THE BRITISH NEWSPAPER LIBRARY
17.

GUILDHALL LIBRARY
40, 53, 57.

THE LONDON DUNGEON
44.

ALL OTHER PICTURES FROM THE AUTHOR'S COLLECTION

ACKNOWLEDGEMENTS

I would like to thank Derrick Spence who has produced some excellent artwork for the last three books, his positive approach is most encouraging. Steve Arnold, when not attending Chesterfield F.C. matches, went through the text with a red pen and was most constructive in his criticism. I received a tick at the end of the book.

Most thanks must go to the wicked people who bought the earlier books in the series, including Terry Sullivan of Sutton, who threatened me with a butcher's knife between the shoulder blades if I did not send him a copy of this book. Don't worry Terry, it's on the way.

HAVE YOU STOPPED BEATING YOUR WIFE?
Domestic violence in Victorian London

1. *Wives were forced to defend themselves from brutish husbands with whatever came to hand.*

EIGHT BLACK EYES

Mrs Seares made the following statement in an East End police station less than twenty-four hours before her death in 1889.

'I, Sarah Seares, am 32 years of age and live at 32, Cadiz St., Stepney. My husband's name is James Seares and we have been married ten years. If I was on the point of death I would make the very same statement I am now going to make.

Last Wednesday I was coming upstairs with some potatoes. No one except my husband, my little boy and girl were in the room. My husband said.

'Why the . . . . did you not come home at the time you said?'

I said 'I met Mrs James and went home with her to see little Johnnie. He is very bad.'

He would not wait for me to say anymore, but hit me in the eye with his fist.

I said 'You don't like to be hit'.

I then picked up the sugar basin and aimed it at him, at the same time saying.

'How do you like that?'

He did nothing else but threw water at me. He then picked up his belt and struck me about the ribs with the buckle-end of it. He used it many times. As he punched me in the right eye, the blow felled me to the ground, and while down he kicked me all over the left part of the body . . .

I never prosecuted him before. I have had some seven black eyes in seven months and have led this life for the past three years. That is all I can say'.

Mrs Seares then made her mark.

Mr Seares made his later in the evening, inflicting his wife's eighth black eye in as many months. The neighbour heard the familiar row with the husband calling his wife 'a bad name', ordering her to make the beds before the regular monthly assault.

When Mrs Seares' body was discovered the next day the police immediately arrested her husband, and charged him with the killing. After a post-mortem however, it was discovered that Mrs Seares' miserable existence had been terminated by natural causes. James was later tried for assault and sentenced to three months hard labour.

The same month Violet Cronk, 20, a maidservant, received the same sentence. Her crime: stealing 3s 6d from her employer.

2. Trivial disputes often led to serious injury.

'For God's sake what are you doing? Leave off throwing that woman around ... you are frightening my children into fits.'

A plea from one Victorian slum dweller to his neighbour, more for peace and quiet than peace of mind. Domestic rows leading to violence were accepted as the norm in the squalid, overcrowded conditions of the East End. In the 1850's most women were dependent on their husbands' income and disputes would often arise over how the family budget should be spent. The choice was usually between food and beer, the husband consuming the ale and then complaining his wife provided him with no supper. One wife, a regular receiver of beatings for not providing food, illustrated the plight of many Victorian mothers.

'He earns twenty shillings a week, and out of that he gives me the odd seven shilling to keep house and food and buy everything.'

Feeling herself entitled to more than the pittance he donated to the family income, Mary Ann Ford stole her husband's weekly wage. She was confronted with the following argument.

'I have treated you kindly all day and you have robbed me of my week's hard earnings.'

Mary Ann was promptly battered to death by her outraged husband.

The cruelty shown to wives was not simply restricted to beating: they might be pushed down the stairs, obliged to let their husband 'have his way' a few days after childbirth, raped or sodomised.

Some wives passively accepted the domination of brutish husbands, others gave as good as they got, defending themselves with whatever came to hand; pokers, knives, walking sticks or umbrellas. When no weapons could be found the tugging of a husband's whiskers and the two traditional means of defence, biting and scratching, prevented many a beating. On odd occasions the contents of a full chamber pot might be emptied over an attacker. One husband had to keep all the cutlery under the bed lest his wife should attack him with her favourite weapons: a knife and fork.

When a battered wife did go to the police to complain about her husband, she was often persuaded to drop the case. Justice Brett observed:

'The women who had been barbarously used, knocked to pieces almost, would say nothing about it. Having been near death's door, they lied to shield the men who so grossly ill-used them.'

The 'persuasion' used was mostly the threat of further violence. One husband said that he would be hanged for her if she appeared against him in court i.e. hanged for her murder. Another husband threw acid in his wife's face and a third simply uttered.

'You . . . . . ., you want to swear my life away.'

He then stabbed his loved one to death.

Not all disputes ended with such brutality. On most occasions either husband or wife, and sometimes both, were the worse for drink when the offences took place. In the cold sober light of day, perceived through the odd black eye, the victim could see no benefit in convicting their relations or friends, these squabbles not being considered police business.

A DROP OF DRINK

'Edward Kelley, 30, costermonger, was charged with violently assaulting his wife, Charlotte Kelley, in Beresford Street, Woolwich—His wife, however, said that she would not press the charge as they had both had a drop of drink, and the prisoner was discharged.'

What led to so many Londoners getting blind-drunk whenever they had a few pennies in their pocket? Probably the main reason was the appalling home conditions that led them to the pub in the first place and into a better environment at least for a few hours.

Jack London describes the sort of home the offender lived in, and this some seventeen years after the above offences:

'As home-life vanishes, the public house appears. Not only do men and women abnormally crave drink, who are overworked, exhausted, suffering from deranged stomachs and bad sanitation, and deadened by the ugliness and monotony of existence, but the gregarious men and women who have no home-life flee to bright and clattering public-houses in a vain attempt to express their gregariousness. And when a family is housed in one small room, home-life is impossible.

A brief examination of such a dwelling will serve to bring to light one important cause of drunkenness. Here the family arises in the morning, dresses and makes its toilet, father, mother, sons and daughters, and in the same room, shoulder to shoulder (for the room is small), the wife and mother cooks the breakfast. And in the same room, heavy and sickening with the exhalations of their packed bodies throughout the night, that breakfast is eaten. The father goes to work, the elder children go to school or into the street, and the mother remains with her crawling, toddling youngsters to do her housework—still in the same room. Here she washes the clothes, filling the pent place with soapsuds and the smell of dirty clothes, and overhead she hangs the wet linen to dry.

Here in the evening, amid the manifold smells of the day, the family goes to its virtuous couch. That is to say, as many as possible pile into the one bed (if bed they have), and the surplus turns in on the floor. And this is the round of their existence, month after month, year after year, for they never get a vacation save when they are evicted. When a child dies, and some are always bound to die, since fifty-five per cent of the East End children die before they are five years old, the body is laid out in the same room. And if they are very poor, it is kept for some time until they can bury it. During the day it lies on the bed; during the night when the living take the bed, the dead occupies the table, from which, in the morning, when the dead is put back into the bed, they eat their breakfast. Sometimes the body is placed on the shelf which serves as a pantry for their food. Only a couple of weeks ago, an East End woman was in trouble because, in this fashion, being unable to bury it, she had kept her dead child three weeks.

The 'honeymoon period' did not last long in some marriages as men tried to lay down ground rules. This case is from Woolwich in 1875;

'Mrs White (wife of prisoner) said her husband came home the previous evening, locked the door, and, taking up a table knife, threatened to stab her, and in attempting to do so he broke the knife. Witness then jumped out of the window to the ground. She had only been married to him for five weeks. He had beaten her before, and on Thursday threw a hob-nailed boot at her. He was very much addicted to drinking.

'Respectable' witnesses would be called to determine which party was telling the truth, in this case the landlady where the prisoner lodged gave evidence:

'He behaved very well to her the first week of their married life, but since that had beat her, and they quarrelled the previous day, because she would not give him her wedding ring to pledge.'

Mr Balguy passing judgement on the prisoner said he felt ashamed that such a fellow should bear the name of man. He sentenced him to a total of nine months imprisonment. The prisoner 'seemed astonished at the sentence, and his mother was carried away fainting.'

A much more lenient punishment was determined North of the River fourteen years later. After pulling all the clothes off his wife, forcing her to eat filth and breaking the complete set of household crockery, Michael Maloney was sentenced to two months hard labour. His wife was given a judicial separation with the defendant having to pay her 12s. weekly.

3. *The first of many beatings one month after marriage.*

A MONTH AFTER MARRIAGE

4. *The lucky ones. Fifty-five per cent of East End children died before the age of five.*

Drink was a factor in most cases of wifebeating though there were other reasons. A wife's refusal to carry out her husband's demands led to many a bruising. Not having dinner on the table when a spouse arrived home could result in fisticuffs. A wife was sent to fetch some boots from the menders. When she returned empty-handed, the repairs not yet effected, the husband proceeded to batter her, later telling the judge he was annoyed at the boots not being finished.

When a wife sent a neighbour's child for her husband's beer instead of going herself he smashed a bottle over her head, later justifying his actions by saying he was particular about sending her for beer to one house.

Wives would resent having to pawn any of their few possessions so their husbands could drink themselves under the table. Mrs Brick's husband insisted that she take her wedding ring off so he might pledge it and get more drink. When she refused she was subjected to a verbal torrent of abuse followed by the husband breaking open her chest of clothes so that he could pawn a gown. Mrs Brick's attempts to prevent her husband stealing the garment resulted in her receiving a blow from a chopper to the head and being dragged out into the street.

One of the most dangerous 'offences' a wife could commit was to embarrass her husband in front of his drinking friends. Harry Wellard's wife sought him out in the local and interrupted his flirting with another woman. She implored him to come home but no sooner had they got outside the pub than he kicked her, causing her to fall to the ground and then put the boot in.

The sole defence offered in the Woolwich magistrates court was that Harry had come home the previous day to find his wife drunk and no tea ready. A policeman who witnessed the scene outside the pub at 1 a.m. stated that both parties were drunk and Harry was bound over for the sum of £5 to keep the peace for three months.

Most husbands had double standards. Drinking was okay for the men but frowned upon in their wives who were expected to provide all their homely comforts. A labourer explained after beating his wife to death:

'If she had stopped at home, instead of going out drinking, it would not have happened.'

Even marriages that appeared successful, at least as far as the neighbours were concerned, might be ruined if one partner or the other over-indulged. The fatal consequences of a drop too much are revealed in Timothy Sullivans' confession in court in June 1882.

'I had a dispute with my wife. I laid down on the floor and my boy pulled my boots off. I laid down again, when my wife said,
"What a wretch you are to be like this every day."

I said: 'Never mind, that's nothing, we will get over all this.'

She said: 'What are you jawing about now?'

I replied: 'I am jawing about nothing.'

She said: 'Hold your jaw.'

I answered: 'Hold your noise or I'll give you this.' I was seated by the fire when I seized a poker and flung it at her. It struck her on the head and she fell backwards. I did not intend to do it.'

The defendant upon hearing of his wife's death later in the day continued;

'I had no right to do it. She was too good a wife. It was a flat sort of iron with a head on it; not a proper poker. I flung it back-handed at her but I did not do it intentionally. She was as good a woman as ever walked the ground. I have been married twenty-three years and never lifted a hand to her. She asked me why I did not turn the drink up, and I said I would.'

After witnesses were called to testify that Mr Sullivans had not been a regular wife-beater, he was found guilty of manslaughter.

An impression as to the types of violence occurring almost every day in South East London is quoted below. The magistrates would hear hundreds of these cases every year and had the difficult task of telling fact from fiction. The details are from the Kentish Independent of 1883.

James Martin, of Powis Street, Woolwich, was summonsed for assaulting his wife on the 5th of April—Eliza Martin said that the defendant, her husband, on the night in question at about 12 o'clock, after they had gone to bed, spat in her face several times, calling her foul names at the same time. She tried to escape from the room as he threatened *'to do'* for her. He told her to get into bed again but she said she was not going to stay there to be murdered by him and called out at the same time trying to pull him away from the door so that she might get out, but he forced something into her mouth and saying:

'Now I'll kick your . . . . . . ribs in.'

5. *Beresford Square, Woolwich. The scene of many late night drunken disputes.*

kicked her in the side twice, fracturing her ribs, owing to which she had to keep to her bed for twelve days. The defendant had no boots on at the time, and was quite sober. The defendant cross-examined his wife as to whether she was sober or not, and as to what she had done with £7 13s. that he had given her that day—to which his wife made answer that she was quite sober and that he had only given her £6 10s., nearly all of which she had expended on paying debts.

Their daughter later remonstrated with her father:

'You old beast, you ought to be ashamed of yourself.'

But he told her to *'hold her tongue'* as he was going to *'give himself up'* for doing it. The defendant said that he went home very unwell and found his wife had been drinking and was very quarrelsome. He went to bed to prevent any disturbance, but on her coming to bed she kept pushing him about, telling him to *'go over further'* (Laughter). He went as far as he could, and told her he could go no further, when she threatened him with the poker. She got out of bed, as he thought, to get the poker, and he got out also to prevent her form obtaining it, and it was in trying to get her into bed again that she must have hurt her ribs. Police Constable Short stated that he had seen Mrs Martin the worse for drink. Mr Martin was reputed to be a very good man when sober, but violent when he had anything to drink. He had been suffering from paralysis and it was thought that he was not quite right in the head. He was at the Seaman's Hospital at Greenwich when the summons was served on him.

Mr Balguy said he thought there were faults on both sides. He thought Mrs Martin had provoked her husband and he did not think there was any intention on his part to break her ribs.

Defendant must find bail of £5 to keep the peace for three months.

THE SOUND OF BREAKING GLASS

Emma Evans was summonsed for breaking ten panes of glass. Henry Evans, her husband, was charged with assault. Mr Balguy was the magistrate presented with the following story:-

Henry had turned his wife out of their home some four months previously because of her misconduct with other men. He had kept the children and moved his mother in to keep house for them.

Emma had returned to the home to effect a reconciliation, but after knocking at the door, she heard it being bolted by one of her own children following the instructions of their grandmother. Emma took great exception to being locked out of her own home and gained entry after breaking a window near the back door. So incensed was she that an orgy of window breaking ensued, terrifying both her mother-in-law and the children. When Henry returned he threw her out into the street.

The marriage had been in trouble for some time. Henry had twice dragged his wife to the police station in the early hours of the morning concerning domestic disputes but the police showed little interest. Emma claimed that Henry would take the law into his own hands but there were no witnesses to substantiate the accusations. She stated that he had slapped her face and thrown her onto an iron rail, nearly breaking her back.

Since the break-up the pair had met at Charing Cross where he had made filthy allusions and spat in her face.

Mr Balguy then asked for Henry's side of the story but was outraged at the proposed defence.

Henry Evans: *'I have one of the children here who could tell you what he has seen of his mother.'* (bringing forward a boy about twelve years old).

Mr Balguy: *'Do you call yourself a man? You ought to be ashamed of yourself to set up a child to give evidence against its mother.'*

After further disclosures showing that Henry had returned Christmas cards and letters with 'disgusting writing' on them to his wife, Mr Balguy saw red. He said he would not dirty his mouth by reading aloud the writing and told Evans he was a dirty beast and ought to be ashamed of himself. He hoped his wife had a brother who would give him a good thrashing. The case was adjourned.

Then as now small domestic affairs would get out of hand and result in serious consequences. When a wife bought a pair of boots with the rent money, she was stabbed by her husband.

Another man who objected to his wife owning a pair of boots was summonsed on a charge of assault. The 40-year-old Hill locked his wife in their Woolwich home on Sunday morning and beat her with a strap until she was black and blue all over the arms, shoulders and back. The beatings had been a weekly occurrence over the last three months since Hill had started seeing a young woman who had lodged in the same house. Since she had moved to central London, the wife-beater would visit her two or three times a week, spending the whole of the family income supporting the new love in his life—Mary.

In defence, Hill said that he had given his wife money and the only reason she had been beaten was because she got between himself and their son, who he was chastising and must have accidentally received 'two or three stripes.'

Calling the defendant a great coward, Mr Balguy committed Hill to hard labour for four months.

AN EXTRAORDINARY CASE

7. *Emma smashed all the windows after being locked out of her own home.*

6. *Kensington High Street. The sort of photo where you notice something new every time you look at it. (See pages 10–11).*

8. *The Boys in Blue, 1887. Many cases of assault upon the police came to court around this time.*

MAY TO NOVEMBER

Patrick Lawlor, a widower aged about seventy, was soon to become disillusioned following his wedding to a youthful bride which had caused a lot of friction within his first family. He was brought before the court on a charge of assaulting his young wife, Emma, in 1883. The magistrate appeared genuinely shocked by the difference in age of the married couple.

Mr Balguy: (to the defendant) *'Is that the man you summonsed?'*

Mrs Lawlor: *'Yes. Sir.'*

Mr Balguy: *'What relation is he to you—your grandfather?'* (Laughter).

Mrs Lawlor: *'My husband, sir.'*

The charge against Patrick Lawlor was that he, with the help of his daughter, had pulled his wife out of bed and punched her in the eye. The reason proffered was that Patrick had just found out about her 'wicked' past. Patrick not surprisingly, told a different tale. He argued that his wife was out all day getting drunk, though he was surprised that she had the money to imbibe to such an extent. He alleged that she took up the tea-kettle and then threatened to throw it at him. Emma then picked up a shovel and it was in the skirmish over this weapon that it 'might have touched her'. Eliza, Patrick's daughter confirmed this story saying that her 'stepmother', who was probably younger than herself, 'abused her fearfully, calling her dreadful names.'

Mr Balguy: *'What business had an old man like you to marry a girl like that?'*

Mr Lawlor: *'That's where I was taken in, sir.'*

Mr Balguy: *'You must pay a fine of 20s. and 2s. costs.'*

This was not however the end of the case. It appears that Patrick did not pay the fine and spent fourteen days in prison. They were back in the same court a few months later.

When Emma, the young wife, returned home Patrick asked her:

'Well, you have not gone yet my . . . . . . flamer?'*

He then once again struck her in the face and she fell down two stairs. Eliza, the daughter, was once again present, and threw her stepmother's hat and jacket after her into the road.

Patrick denied ever lifting a hand to his wife, but revealed his true dissatisfaction with his young bride when he said that he did not know that she had four or five bastards when he married her.

Mr Balguy was genuinely opposed to this 'May to November' marriage.

Mr Balguy: *'But you knew she was a young woman.'*

Mr Lawlor: *'Why she draws half-a-crown a week now for one of the kids.'* (Laughter).

Mr Balguy: *'That's all the better for you.'* (Laughter).

Mr Lawlor: *'But she only gets drunk with the money.'*

—Mr Balguy ordered the defendant to find bail of £5 to keep the peace for three months.

*A flamer is an old word for prostitute. The blank does not need a great deal of guessing for those with an alliterative mind.

'PECULIAR PEOPLE'

Assault cases did not always follow the pattern of drunken husbands beating wives with the nearest blunt instrument. Henry Hines, a member of the religious sect known as 'the Peculiar People' was summonsed by his wife for assault although both agreed that he never struck her. The case was peculiar in more ways than one.

After twenty seven years of marriage, Henry had had enough. His main interest in life was now his religious work with the Peculiar People, he rejected his wife for being ungodly as she would not wear the garb or follow the ways of his sect. Henry had particularly objected to his wife's headwear which he condemned as 'a bad women's bonnet' and was in the habit of preaching her down for the evil life she led. He had taken the children to be looked after by the 'Peculiar sisters' and stated that he would not return them until she led a godly life.

Henry finally decided to leave home and as he was collecting his clothes his wife clung to him pleading with undying loyalty:

'Where you go, I go.'

Mrs Hines then alleged that he thrust her away and pinched and squeezed her which hurt very much.

In his defence Henry complained that his wife neglected both himself and his home, insulted him in public, followed him and annoyed him when he visited the dying and sick and cared little for their children. He claimed that he had not raised a finger to her throughout their married life. Mr Marsham, judging the case, tried to get the couple together again:

Mr Marsham: *'Can you not make it up and remain at home with her in peace?'*

Defendant: *'It is impossible. I will go anywhere from her to be at rest.'*

Complainant: *'You hate me because I won't wear ugly bonnets, and you won't be seen with me in the streets for fear of those "Peculiar People." Give me 5s. a week and you may go.'*

Defendant: *'No; I have to keep the two children, and you can keep yourself.'*

Complainant: *'Make it 4s. 6d..'*

Defendant: *'Not another penny. I would sooner go to the end of the world.'*

Complainant: *'A good job if you went, and you would get rid of your tutors'* (Laughter). *'Sign your paper, I'll take the 4s..'*

Mr Marsham adjourned the case for a month in order that separation might be arranged.

After the change of law in 1857, cruelty which did not involve physical violence upon the wife, was recognised as good grounds for divorce. If a father mistreated the children in front of his wife, or treated her in the street as if she were a common prostitute these offences were seen as the grossest and most abominable cruelty. Other offences were: regular drunkenness, carousing with the servant, entertaining prostitutes and drunkenly urinating throughout the house.

MORNING COFFEE

In the Baker v Baker divorce of 1863 Emma sued her husband Tom partly because of the violent altercations they had experienced over a fairly long period, but also for his unreasonable behaviour. It was one of the first cases of its kind since the change in the divorce law.

Emma complained that her husband would stay out until the early hours, returning about 4 a.m. and expect his wife to get up and make coffee for both himself and a friend. The judge agreed that this was an excessive demand, though Tom and his counsel were both shocked by the ruling.

'SCOLDING, SCOLDING, SCOLDING'

Mental cruelty takes a great deal longer to heal than a swift punch or kick often delivered in an alcoholic state and very much regretted the next day. Mrs Curtis had to endure physical abuse early after her marriage to John in 1846 but the beatings stopped and a new, far more cruel approach was adopted by the husband to subordinate his wife.

Frances was shown up on every occasion that John felt she had done something wrong and made to look a fool in front of the servant. Let's leave Frances to take up the story:

'He went on perpetually at me the whole evening; next, he made me beg his pardon over again in the presence of my servant, explaining to her that I had been impertinent to him . . . then this morning there had been the same thing over again,—scolding, scolding, scolding without end, and I can conscientiously say without provocation, pointedly helping the servant to bread at breakfast before me, and at last, on my making some remark, sending me out of the room to finish my breakfast in my bedroom.'

John then forbade his wife to see their children. When they entered the room *'he sent them off, telling them repeatedly that mamma was naughty'* Frances was so desperate to end the marriage that she secretly hoped her husband would strike her to facilitate a divorce;

'but that he never attempts,—indeed, he seemed much kinder for a while; but the plain fact is that he carries the idea of his authority to a mania.'

The judge found for Frances Curtis, recognising that cruelty need not always involve physical violence.

NAGGED, TAUNTED AND INSULTED

What induced men to behave in such a brutal manner? In their own defence husbands would argue that they had been aggravated. 'She was very quarrelsome and used aggravating words.' Men particularly objected to being nagged, taunted, insulted or having their role as head of the house contested. They also very much disapproved of their wives spending excessive amounts of time with female friends or relations. The double standards were in evidence again when so many husbands objected to their wives swearing. Any challenge had to be stifled, Mrs Broom relates what happened when she challenged her husband.

9. *The real victims of warring parents. East End children outside the local pub.*

'*A few words passed between me and my husband. He said if I said anymore he would slap me in the face with a piece of bacon he had in his hand. I said that was more than he dare do—then he gave me a smack in the face with the back of his hand.*'

The son who witnessed the altercation gave a different account.

'*Mother and father had a row. Mother was calling father names—she called him a bastard whoremonger and tried to scratch his face.*'

DANGEROUS SLEEPING PARTNERS

The use of violence was far more common amongst the working classes and outraged some members of the press. Wife-beaters were called '*brutes*', '*ruffians*' and '*tyrants*' with the Times editorial stating that '*these monsters outrage every law of civilized man, and violate every instinct of human nature.*'

The judiciary, all men, reacted in different ways, probably according to their own individual relationships with women. Some seemed to have sympathy with certain wife-beaters. Edward Cox who gave advice on sentencing in his handbook 'Principles of Punishment' hinted that some wives were not as innocent as they would like to have the courts believe. He would portray the bad wife as a woman who:

'*has made her husband's home an earthly hell, who spends his earnings in drink, pawns his furniture, starves her children, provides for him no meals, lashes him with her tongue when sober and with her fists when drunk, and if he tries to restrain her fits of passion, resists with a fierceness and a strength for which he is no match. He is labouring all day to feed and clothe her and his children, and when he returns home at night, this is his greeting.*'

As we have seen, the cards were very strongly stacked against women in Victorian London. In 1859, there was an altercation in Greenwich between Samuel Newbury and his wife. The judge dismissed the case saying that there was equal blame on both sides. Mrs Newbury had thrown a hairbrush at her husband; Mr Newbury had tried to stab his wife.

Even the police, at times, were in a no-win situation. In 1871 a police officer was convicted of common assault and fined, after preventing a man from beating his wife, as the magistrate believed that a woman was the property of her husband.

Some magistrates would hear no bad against the woman defining a wife-beater as 'one of those cowardly fellows who thought he had a perfect right to knock about his wife as he thought proper.'

The sentences meted out depended a great deal on the 'machoness', or otherwise, of the magistrate.

The number of reported cases of wife-beating fell between 1850 and 1890 though whether this was due to greater understanding between the sexes, or thrashings continuing in private, is unsure. Even today the police are reluctant to intervene in a 'domestic', lest both sides round on them.

CRIMES AGAINST THE PERSON
Child-beating, common assault and sexual crime

10. *Societies for the protection of children were founded to counter the horrific cruelty of some parents.*

'DADDA DID IT WITH A STRAP'

The chastisement of children with a clip or cuff around the ear was such an everyday occurrence that few people bothered to complain about it. The child would just accept the punishment for being caught and go about his everyday business. As we have seen with the wife-beaters, some, especially drunken men, displayed a nasty streak of violence which often led to serious injury to their offspring.

The casual attitude displayed by many child-beaters indicated that they thought their actions had been perfectly normal.

'I did thrash it. When I came home on Monday my wife told me the child had stolen a piece of bacon, so I beat her with a strap, as I thought I was justified in correcting her.'

Inspector Pearson confirmed that he was, as long as the correction was not too severe. He then examined the girl and found on the lower part of her body one mass of discolouration and bruises. When asked who had caused the injuries the young girl replied, *'Dadda did it with a strap.'* John never denied the charge and produced a round leather strap about a yard and a half long. Little sympathy came from the doctor who confirmed that the young girl had no doubt received a severe beating, but 'she would soon get over it.'

11. *Many children ran away and lived on the streets rather than endure beatings.*

Mrs Powell's attempts to defend her young son from his father were the more remarkable as she was the child's stepmother. When she came between father and son Alfred threatened:

'I will cut his heart out and put it on a dish. If you interfere I will serve you the same.'

The defendant then began assaulting his wife as he had been doing for years, by kicking her. He had never given her any money and she paid the rent and supported herself by working as a cook. Mr Williams agreed there were grounds for a separation and imprisoned Alfred for one day, with the defendant ordered to contribute to his wife's upkeep.

Fortunately, organisations other than the police had begun to investigate cases of child abuse.

In 1887 the London Society for the Prevention of Cruelty to Children had been running for three years and its report displays the brutal facts of existence for thousands of defenceless young children. Some of the cases they investigated included the following:

Strapping a deaf and dumb boy because it was extremely difficult to make him undersand; drawing a red-hot poker before the eyes of a blind girl and touching her with it (this was done by her brother, in the presence of her parents and for fun); after beating, locking up for the night in a coal-cellar with rats; immersing a dying baby in a tub of cold water for nearly an hour 'to get this dying done'; breaking a girl's arm while beating her with a broomstick, then setting her to scrub the floor with the broken arm folded to her breast, and whipping her for being so long about it; hanging a naked boy by tied hands from a hook in the ceiling, there flogging him; savagely beating with loin-belt, felling with fist, and then kicking in the groin, on the abdomen and face with working boots; lashing a three-

year-old face and neck with a drayman's whip; a three-year-old back beaten with whalebone riding-whip; throttling a boy, producing partial strangulation to stop his screams of pain; beating on scarcely-healed old sores, then thrusting the nob of a poker into the lad's throat, and holding it there to stop the row.

Children might be kept starving for one of two reasons: their parents were totally indifferent as to what became of them, or they deliberately tried to kill them. Children would be left locked up in cold, dark and damp rooms without food, whilst their parents went to work or, more likely, to the pub.

The London Society gave details of one of the many cases investigated:

'When found, the child sat in the passage on the bare oilcloth, alone, hungry and cold, shivering and ill, in nothing but its night-gown. It was the depth of winter; a through draught ran from the front door to the back. On the other side of the door, opening into the passage was a room with a fire, and a breakfast table spread, and that child's mother sitting at it, eating a meal of hot coffee, frizzled bacon and bread. The child had been deliberately placed, and left where it was by that mother. She had then gone in to her own breakfast, and shut the door. The child could not get up, could not even stand, it was five years old and insured for £7.'

Other cases quoted concerned 'a five year old dried-up skeleton' with facial bruising called 'a little devil' by dad. In another case, a father would take refreshments during the intervals between beating his children. A third ordered his daughter upstairs to strip ready for punishment. He had a little nap and when he arrived at the room found his daughter had committed suicide by throwing herself from the bedroom window.

12. *Poor but happy.*

13. *Toffs take on the local louts.*

Although wife-beating was one of the most prevalent forms of assault, very few people were safe wandering the streets after the pubs had been open for a few hours. Cases of assault filled pages of all the London local newspapers, though once again many charges were dropped if the victim knew his or her assailant. The following two accounts were heard in Woolwich; one north of the river, the other a short ferry ride away. The only punishment a magistrate could impose was to bind over the offender to keep the peace for a period of months.

BITING A WOMAN'S EAR

Michael Driscoll, 28, was charged with willfully assaulting Ann Slater, by biting off a piece of her ear.

The prosecutrix said the previous afternoon the prisoner who lodged in her house got quarrelling with her brother, a soldier just returned from India. They were going to fight, and the witness got between them, when the prisoner threw her down and bit a piece off her ear. He was, however, the worse for drink, and she did not wish to press the charge against him.

ASSAULT WITH A POKER

'George Galloway, 62, was charged with assaulting Louisa Mullins, by striking her on the head with a poker; and Henry Galloway 21, of the same address, was charged with assaulting his father, the first named prisoner. Louisa Mullins said that she lived with her mother in the same house as the prisoners. On Saturday night,

about half past twelve, the elder prisoner had been quarrelling with his son, and he struck her on the head with the poker produced. She gave him no provocation for doing so, and she did not know why he did it. His eyesight was very bad and she did not know whether he struck her intentionally or not. She wished to withdraw from the charge if his worship would bind the prisoner over to keep the peace.

George Galloway was then put in the witness box, but he refused to say anything against his son, he hoped "the Lord would never forgive him" if he did. He denied having any knowledge of striking the female with the poker.'

Mr Balguy: *'Why did you have the poker in your hand?'*

Witness: *'I was going to fasten my door.'*

Mr Balguy: *'Do you fasten your door with a poker?'* (Laughter)

Witness: *(in a whining tone)* *'Why I always fasten it with a poker; nothing else to do it with, Sir.'* (Laughter)

Police Constable Rutherford, 227R, said he was called to 3, Cock Yard, by the female witness, and took the prisoners into custody. The elder prisoner was bleeding from the effects of a kick in the back inflicted by his son. The surgeon was called to him as well as to Louisa Mullins, a fee of 7s. 6d. being incurred in each case. Mr Balguy bound the prisoners in the sum of £5 to keep the peace for three months.

London suffered two great panics over the fear of street violence in 1856 and 1862, these fears in many ways were made much worse by the influence of the press. The panics were a reaction to the supposed increase in cases of 'garotting', a method of robbery 'involving, the crushing of the throat leaving the victim on the ground writhing in agony, with tongue protruding and eyes staring from their sockets, unable to give the alarm or attempt a pursuit.'

Victims would usually be attacked at night by gangs, one member approaching the victim from behind and the forearm brought across the Adam's apple to cut off the air supply, with the others stealing anything they could lay their hands on from the victim's pockets. There were a number of reports of such attacks in 1856 and the press attributed the increase in street crime to the release on a kind of parole or, 'ticket-of-leave', of convicts who would normally have been transported to Australia, now refusing to accept any more felons.

The Times was primarily responsible for the large amount of publicity relating to garotting when it stated that a man cannot walk:

'without imminent danger of being throttled, robbed, and if not actually murdered, at least kicked and pommelled within an inch of his life.'

Amongst the thirty-one letters published by the Times on the subject in 1856 was one from 'The London Scoundrel':

'Away with maudlin sympathy and twaddle. When a ruffian watches you at night, fractures your skull, lacerates your windpipe, or clogs your brain with apoplectic blood, hang him, if you are lucky enough to catch him. Shoot him at the time if you can, but, if not, hang him!'

The real reason for the panic was that footpads were becoming a lot bolder, and street crime was not now just confined to the poorest areas but had spread to the most frequented thoroughfares of the capital. Both rich and poor were now affected and when the MP for Blackburn was robbed in Pall Mall in the summer of 1862, a second garotting panic ensued.

Jokes were printed in Punch showing two law-abiding citizens setting about each other to pre-empt an assault and cartoons about citizens attacking trees in the fog appeared, but there was also serious concern. New penal settlements to receive prisoners were considered with The Falkland Islands and Cameroon Mountains discussed. There was a popular demand for more floggings with the main long-term outcome of the panics being the Prisons Act of 1856 which made the conditions within the gaols even harsher, encouraging beatings with the birch and lashings with the cat-o'-nine-tails.

14. *The lout's revenge.*

15. *The sentence for premeditated rape by two young men was three months imprisonment.*

SEXUAL ASSAULTS

Just one hundred years ago, sexual assault was not considered nearly as serious a crime as it is today. Indeed incest was not criminalised until 1908 and fathers could legally have sex with their 13-year-old daughters before the age of consent was raised in the 1880's. If the daughter objected, and the case somehow brought to court, it was nearly always dismissed because the daughter showed insufficient resistance.

Without the help of forensic science the outcome of most Victorian rape cases depended on whether the judge and jury believed the victim or the accused. Rape victims were terribly disadvantaged by those judging them being all male, and holding the hypocritical prejudices of the time. Women suffered simply through being female, by not being under the supervision of a male guardian, and openly admitting in court that they had lost their sexual 'innocence', although through no fault of their own. If a woman did anything less than put up a violent struggle against her assailant this implied that the act had not been against her will. The evidence for struggle would often depend on the severity of the victim's injuries; if few were visible, the chances for acquital were greater.

If the rapist fled the scene and the victim reported the case immediately there was a greater chance of prosecution. The rape of domestic servants by the householder, his son, or friends, was rarely reported, as the victim could find herself without home or job. If a case looked like going to court, the victim would be offered a bribe to drop the action which many accepted. If the case was proceeded with the charge of rape was extremely difficult to prove, with most convictions being for indecent assault.

Under the headline 'Disgraceful assault' the following report is taken from the City Press of 1871. Many readers may be surprised at the sentence.

'James Day, 18, and Charles Hart, 16 years of age, described as glass-blowers, were charged with an aggravated assault. The complainant was a young woman of 29, employed as a cook at the King's Head and Lamb Tavern, in Upper Thames Street. About 8 o'clock on Sunday evening she was crossing Tower Hill on her way home, and was followed by the prisoners. In Upper Thames Street the prisoners suddenly rushed from a passage and, seizing her, drew her into it and threw her upon the ground. As she lay the prisoner Day committed a grossly indecent assault upon her, and the other held his hand over her mouth to prevent her screaming. She shouted as well as she could, but no one came to her assistance. The younger prisoner, Hart, afterwards tried to assault her in like manner but she successfully resisted notwithstanding that Day, who then assisted in holding her down, threatened to disfigure her if she moved. They at length left her in an exhausted state, and on recovering she complained to the first policeman she met. Later in the evening the prisoners were apprehended from a description she gave of them, and afterwards identified them at the Bow Lane Police Station. They were both drunk. The Lord Mayor said the prisoners had behaved in a disgraceful and ruffianly way on this occasion and he sentenced each of them to three months hard labour.'

16. *Many rape charges were never brought to court. A bribe or threat usually did the job.*

Probably the main factor which influenced the all male judiciary was the status of the female complainant. A young girl who had been 'forbidden the door' by the new man in her mother's life and been found wandering the streets, had very little chance of being believed. Sarah Wilson was offered a room in Sarah Phillpott's house after both she and her husband had taken pity on the homeless servant. The thirteen-year-old bought a charge against a fellow lodger, Matt Horn, a thirty-two-year-old labourer, who had resided with the Phillpotts for six months, and slept in a backroom with their two little boys. The alleged offence took place in Plumstead in 1885.

'The prosecutrix said that on Sunday morning about six o'clock, the prisoner came into her bedroom, undressed and rubbed his face against hers. She cried and told him to go out of the room. He shook hands with her, and told her not to tell anyone, and went out of the room. Witness told her mother the same evening . . .'

Mrs Phillpott, the landlady, continued the story;

On Sunday morning Sarah Wilson came down and had breakfast with both herself and her family, but not a word of the alleged charge was mentioned by the girl . . . During the whole of the time the prisoner had lived with her, she had always found him a thoroughly decent and respectable man. She thought it quite likely that he might have gone into the girl's room to look into the street, without thinking of her being there.

Mr Balguy told the prisoner that, in his opinion, there was not the slightest foundation for the charge preferred against him, and ordered him to be discharged.

Dr Ralph Hodgson came up with some original treatments at his Greenwich practice. When a servant girl, Agnes Bailey, went to his surgery still suffering from the effects of gas administered during a tooth extraction one week previously, she had not expected to have her breasts massaged. The doctor stated that gas caused weakness of the heart, and during an examination of her chest 'acted improperly.' He then went on to assault her more seriously though we are not told his medical reasons for the second course of treatment. Agnes finally screamed and resisted his advances to the utmost before he ejected her from the surgery.

Elizabeth Webb, suffering from indigestion, went to Dr. Hodgson's surgery and received the same treatment, the defendant also kissed her twice and suggested that a ride in his carriage would do her good!

The evidence was considered sufficient to have Dr. Hodgson committed for trial.

For those interested in Victorian crime there is no better source than the Illustrated Police News although this is very difficult to obtain these days. The edition of Saturday, June 10th, has been chosen as it shows the wide variety of offences reported and on this occasion they all took place in the capital, all that is except the encounter with a sea monster!

BOY TIED TO CART WHEEL AND WORRIED BY A DOG

The first illustration is of a boy named Cole. For some time both he and his friends had been tormenting a certain William Jarvis. At the end of his tether one Friday evening the gatekeeper determined to teach the boy a lesson. Running out of his house, he seized young Cole and fastened him with a chain to the wheel of a cart. It was his turn to do the tormenting now. Producing a dog of the pomeranian breed, the tormented man shouted:

'Bite him Jack.'

The dog obeyed the commands and flew at the boy, biting his legs and tearing his clothes. When a girl named Jane Middleton appeared, Jarvis ordered Jack to seize her but she made good her escape and acted as a witness for the prosecution. William Jarvis was fined £5 or suffer a month's imprisonment. The gatekeeper chose the fine.

HORRIBLE TRAGEDY AT FULHAM

The, horrible tragedy at Fulham, was a drunken brawl after two gentlemen and a ladyfriend had been to Epsom to see the Oaks. The fight was probably over the lady, with one of the men smashing a full whisky bottle over the other, and death being caused by haemorrhaging due to stab wounds inflicted with a poultry carving knife.

ENCOUNTER WITH A SEA MONSTER

No, we can't leave it out, here is the story of the encounter with a sea monster: . . . The statement made by the crew is to the effect that while engaged hauling their lines twenty-eight miles east-south-east of Fetlar (Shetlands) they saw at a short distance from them something that had the appearance of three small hillocks, each about the size of a six-oared boat upset, which blew when coming to the surface. It disappeared in the direction of the boat, and shortly afterwards they saw the monster pass underneath the boat. When it came up again it passed right in the direction of the boat, with its mouth wide open—a mouth that to all appearances could have taken in their boat. There seemed to be whiskers of a green colour, and about seven or eight feet long, hanging from its mouth; very large green eyes, and on its head were great lumps about the size of a herring barrel. They threw stones at it, but it still came on towards them and only again disappeared below water when a few yards from the boat, on a charge of swan shot being discharged into its mouth.

MATRIMONIAL TROUBLES

We should turn without further comment to the case of Barstow and matrimonial troubles. The reporter seems to have been enamoured of the tall, middle-aged woman bringing a case against her husband, describing her hairstyle in detail—'with frizzy hair in front and a long corkscrew ringlet hanging from her head behind.' Maybe these details were for the artist who otherwise had to rely a great deal upon his imagination. The woman wanted a separation from her second husband but found herself in the wrong court; nonetheless she told her story, one that is all too familiar.

Her husband, who had been broke when she met him, had stated that he only wanted to make her a kind, loving and affectionate partner and to look after her in her hour of need and professed no interest in the 'flesh pots'. After only five months everything had gone wrong, he had 'thrown off his mask and shown himself in his true colours'. His life was now one long round of drinking and cursing, the ale money being stolen from the till of his wife's business. The woman feared the workhouse unless she could somehow get her husband to leave. The magistrate once again recommended the divorce court but with average costs about £40 per divorce, this way of escape was beyond her means. The magistrate could do little but offer sympathy, not even a cup of tea.

ACCIDENTALLY HANGED

A verdict of death from misadventure was returned after the jury had heard the story of 13-year-old Edward Puller. He had been found hanging from a hatpeg fastened on the back of the bedroom door, a sheet tied around his neck. Very fond of playing with ropes and sheets, he had often deliberately frightened his grandmother. There was no suspicion of foul play and no grounds to support a verdict of suicide.

FATAL SKIPPING, PECKHAM

The 'fatal skipping' case in Peckham featured another life tragically cut short after seven-year-old Alice Lucy Parker fell, whilst skipping with three friends, and later died from concussion.

DOING HIS FOURTEEN DAYS

The fourteen days case is reported in full:
'At Bow Street on Saturday last week, Henry Wilson, whose appearance in the dock in the garb of a convict caused a great deal of amusement, was charged with being drunk and disorderly in High Holborn on Friday night. At about twelve o'clock the defendant had a large crowd around him, and as he was shouting and behaving in a very disorderly manner, Police Constable 155 took him into custody.'

Mr Flowers: (to prisoner) *'Well, what have you to say?'*

Murgatroyd: (the Chief Usher, in a stage whisper) *'He's dressed as a convict, sir.'*

Mr Flowers: (adjusting his spectacles) *'Yes I was just going to see what dress it was. Let me see "Fourteen days." What does it mean? Had he that on when you took him into custody?'* (Laughter).

Constable: *'Yes, sir. It's an advertisement of a new play at the Criterion Theatre.'*

Mr Flowers: (to defendant) *'Why, you see you have had sentence passed on you already. How came you to get drunk?'*

The Defendant said that he had been out all day and had nothing to eat, and as he was going home some gentleman had given him some whisky. Mr Flowers said it would have been better if they had given him something to eat. Of course he (the defendant) was not to blame for going out in the garb, but he must not get drunk again, and with this piece of advice he was discharged, Mr. Flowers hoping that he (defendant) might never have to wear the clothes in any other way.

17. *The gory facts of existence as captured by The Illustrated Police News.*

DANGEROUS WOMEN
An assortment of offences from crimes of violence to shoplifting

HIGHWAY ROBBERY BY WOMEN

18. Skinners at work.

We move now from assaults on women to those by women. The cases of being drunk and disorderly and fighting, though not as numerous as those heard against men, took up a great deal of the court's time. There were undoubtably some hard women about who gave as much, if not more, than they got.

Although mostly a male crime, women were not averse to attacking well-heeled, prosperous-looking gentlemen if they strayed into their territory. What Joseph Masel was doing wandering around the dark alleyways of Spitalfields with £51 in his pocket, we shall never know. Mary Neal, 22,

and an older female accomplice were attracted by the cap-makers's boots, little could they have expected the prize they were to find in his pockets.

Joseph gave his account of the attack saying that he was overpowered by the women, thrown to the ground with Mary putting her hand over his mouth so that he would not cry out. They took the boots off his feet and rifled him, tearing his pockets and removing his purse. Being a teetotaller, Joseph remembered clearly all the events of the evening and later at Commercial Street Police Station, identified Mary without hesitation, although there were three other women present. Mary denied all the charges and only had 6½d. in her possession. She was remanded and the police confident they could find the other woman involved.

THRASHED WITH A HAIRBRUSH

Tears running down both cheeks, Mrs Smith began testifying against her husband on a charge of assault. It soon became plain, however, as to who was the more dominant of the married couple. Robert's wife claimed that he returned home drunk about twelve-thirty and punched her in the eye. He then dragged her out of bed and tore the nightdress off her back.

Mrs Smith was more than a match for her husband, as she demonstrated in her version of the events: 'I gave him a good sound thrashing with a hairbrush—what he had wanted for a long time (Laughter)—and left the marks he showed now, (Mr Smith had a black eye).

Mrs Smith went on to say that she was as good a man as her husband and then called her mother to corroborate her story. In his defence, Mr Smith argued that when he returned home his wife started nagging him about a loan and threw something at him. When he retaliated, her mother and father joined in, holding him down while his wife thrashed him.

Mr Balguy, the magistrate, suggested that the husband got his due rewards but Mr Smith had not given up the case and called a young man, Samuel Webb, to give evidence in his favour. Samuel testified that on an earlier occasion he had accompanied Robert Smith home and had seen his wife push him on the couch and start to punch him, imploring the young man to hold her husband down.

Mrs Smith was livid and pleaded with his worship not to believe the 'infamous lies' of 'an infamous wretch of a boy'. It was only with great difficulty that she was restrained from attacking the young man in court, with many fearing for his safety after proceedings were finished. These thoughts were also going through the magistrate's mind as he gave judgement:

Mr. Balguy: 'That witness had better get out of the way quick, and go home as fast as he can and never look back once (Loud laughter).'

Mr Smith: 'Ah, she's as good as a man, sir.'

Mr Balguy: 'I dare say you deserved what you got. You struck her first. You are bound over in the sum of £5 to keep the peace for three months.'

THE CHEEK OF IT

On Saturday, at Stratford Petty Sessions, Mary Lucy, widow, aged fifty-four, living at Mansfield Road, East Ham, was charged with savagely assaulting Jemima Baker, a married woman, of the same place. The prosecutrix, whose face was enveloped in bandages, deposed that on the night of 17th September 1883, she was returning home by the fields to Bonny Downs when she overtook the prisoner, who, without provocation, abused her and accused her of jealousy. The witness denied the allegation, whereupon the prisoner threw a quart glass bottle containing beer at her. The missile struck her on the left cheek, cutting it open. The prisoner then knocked the witness down, fell upon her, and attempted to bite her nose, but witness turned her face. The prisoner then seized her right cheek by her teeth, and bit it off, filling her mouth with it, and afterwards spitting it onto the ground. Prosecutrix had since been under medical advice. There was no real defence.

The bench characterised it as a brutal and shocking case, and ordered the prisoner—who had been locked up three weeks—to pay a fine of £5 or be imprisoned for two months with hard labour.

BEATEN WITH HIS OWN WOODEN LEG

Thus ran the headline in reports from the Woolwich Police Court 1890. 'Mary Halliday, 32, married, was charged with being drunk and disorderly. Police Constable Baker said that the previous evening the prisoner was drunk and quarrelling with her husband in Albion Road, Woolwich. A crowd of about 100 persons assembled round them, and the tram traffic was stopped. He got her away once, but she returned and renewed her disorderly conduct, and he was obliged to take her into custody.

Prisoner: 'I deny being drunk. I was only having a few words with my husband because he wanted the money I had been at work for all day.'

Mr Kennedy: 'Is anything known about the prisoner?'

Sergt. Gilham: 'Yes, your Worship. She has been summonsed for assaulting her husband, who has a wooden leg. On one occasion she upset him, unshipped his wooden leg, and knocked him about with it.' (Laughter).

Mr Kennedy (to the prisoner): 'You must now pay a fine of 5s. or go to prison for five days.'

A DISRESPECTFUL DAUGHTER

Some birds never quite manage to leave the nest. The parents of a thirty-five-year-old woman took their daughter to court as they seemed to have no control over her behaviour. The father appeared in Thames Police Court his face covered with bandages and sticking plaster, the year 1887. Let's hear some of the testimony:

Father: 'I was a-laying down, your worship, when I heard my daughter say to her mother that "she'd do for her," and I got up to separate them, and she ups with a jug and hits me over my head, and cuts it open. Bled a pint and a half.'

When asked for her side of the story, the daughter said that she was getting her parents' tea ready—

'Crumpets and all,' when she and her mother got somehow to a bit of words, which wouldn't adone any harm, only father he got a interfering, and—she was very sorry indeed—she couldn't make out now how it had all come about as it had.'

Mr Saunders: (the magistrate): 'What is her usual character?'

Father: 'Won't do anything your Worship.'

Mr Saunders: 'Will not work?'

Father: 'Won't do anything—and I can't get rid of her!'

Mr Saunders: 'Has she ever been violent before?'

Father: 'Only a week or so ago she was, sir. She'd been out and got a black eye somewhere, and she came home and said she meant to swear it to me!'

Daughter: 'Oh, father!'

Mr Saunders: 'Seven days.'

SO YOUNG AND PRETTY

Tottie Smith went to the dock in just a striped petticoat and a coloured dress improver at the back. The tall good-looking young woman wore neither shoes nor stockings and her hair was dishevelled. Tottie immediately caught the attention of all those present in the courtroom: proudly wishing the clerk, 'Good morning!' She winked and nudged the gaoler as he went on to tell the magistrate that Tottie had been in the cells from midday, the previous day, not being sober enough to appear.

19. The modest Tottie entertains the court.

Mr D'Eyncourt (to prisoner): 'Are you sober now?'

Prisoner: 'I don't know; do you?'

As the evidence was about to be heard, the prisoner looked appealingly at Mr D'Eyncourt and enquired:

Prisoner: 'Why don't you discharge me, Mr Magistrate? You ought to, for I am so young and pretty (Great laughter). Oh, you are a funny old man, and nice too.' (Roars of laughter).

26

Mr D'Eyncourt: 'Have you had anything to drink this morning?'

Prisoner: 'I've had some water (Laughter) I wanted a "brandy-and-water" poured out till it got cold—(Great laughter)—but the Colonel, who knows me well, wouldn't let me have it. (Renewed laughter). Oh! but why do you keep me here? Why don't you let me go away from here? I am young and really good-looking, am I not? (More laughter). I think you ought to. You don't often see a girl like me.' (Renewed laughter).

The Clerk: 'Be quiet. What is your right name?'

Prisoner: (Smiling) 'I am sure **you** would like to know. I'll tell you—Nelly Thornton!' (Laughter).

(Tottie was one of the many nicknames for a prostitute).

The constable then went on to give evidence as to how he found the prisoner 'ginned-up' and refusing to move on.

Mr D'Eyncourt: 'Did she make use of any bad language?'

Constable: 'No, your Worship.'

Prisoner: 'I never do so. I don't think it nice. (Great laughter). But I was creating a disturbance in the public street, of course I was, according to the evidence of the constable.' (Laughter).

Mr D'Eyncourt: 'Do you wish to ask the constable any questions?'

Prisoner: (smiling and in a satirical manner) 'No, thanks (Laughter) 'it would be no use. Policemen never tell lies (Great laughter) well hardly ever. They couldn't if they tried. You know that, sir.' (Great laughter).

Mr D'Eyncourt: (to the constable) 'Was she disorderly?'

Prisoner: 'How could I be? I was fast asleep.' (More laughter).

The magistrate then enquired if anything was known about the prisoner, the chief gaoler replying that she had once been charged for drunkenness.

Prisoner: 'Wait a minute. Allow me to assist you (Laughter). A few weeks ago I was brought here for knocking on the wrong door. That was a nice sort of thing to drag anybody to the station for, wasn't it? (Roars of laughter). Don't you think I am a very nice young lady?' (More laughter).

Mr D'Eyncourt: 'You are a very foolish young woman to take so much drink.'

Prisoner: 'It's not your fault, I can assure you, sir. Its's not indeed.' (Great laughter).

Mr D'Eyncourt: 'Well, go about your business.'

Prisoner: 'Oh, you are a kind old gentleman! Anyone could like you. (Roars of laughter) But you don't seem to take to me any of you. Well, I can't help it; but I am nice.'

Tottie went straight from the courthouse to the ale house and was re-arrested that very afternoon. At her next appearance she was ordered to the workhouse and blowing kisses to all about her, shouted out,

'Goodbye, you gay dogs. Good luck to you.'

'WOMEN OF MOST REPULSIVE APPEARANCE'

Very little respect was shown towards the bench by the hardened female drinkers and prostitutes of East London. They appeared indifferent to the punishment meted out but would certainly have objected to the East London Advertiser's report on their looks. The hearing took place in 1889, with London still terrified by the stories of Jack the Ripper.

'Mary Anderson, 50, Alice Fox, 35, Johannan Feah, 38, and Mary Ann Dowsett, 28, four women of most repulsive appearance, were charged at the Thames Court with being drunk and disorderly.

Constable Cox said he was in Ratcliff with another officer when he saw the prisoners with two others behaving in a very disorderly manner. They were also using horrible language and pulled passers-by about. Anderson and Feah also started fighting. As they could not get the prisoners away, the witness and the other officer arrested them—in answer to the charge Anderson said she was very unhappy and would not be happy until she found 'Jack the Ripper'.

Mr Lushington said the accused had made themselves a perfect nuisance and they would each be sentenced to one month's hard labour.

Feah: *'Thank you, my old darling. Happy New Year to you.'*

They were removed laughing and shouting.

'SHAN'T SAY ANYTHING BALD HEAD'

Amelia Maelhouse's young man had found himself a new ladyfriend and, seeing no future for himself, the eighteen-year-old determined to commit suicide by swallowing a quantity of paraffin. With the taking of your own life being a criminal offence, Amelia was hauled before the magistrate; she already had a reputation for being rude and impudent, having been remanded for repeatedly telling the magistrate to 'shut up'.

Showing little respect for the court, she stood with her head bowed and when asked to raise it replied,

'Shan't, shan't.'

Stamping her way into the dock Amelia still refused to look at the magistrate but heard the chief clerk enquire;

'Is there any letter this week about the prisoner?'

Amelia: *'Shut up.'*

Mr Lushington (Magistrate): *'What have you got to say this week about attempting to take your life?'*

Amelia: *'Shan't say anything, bald head. I shan't go back.'* (Amelia started to stamp her feet). *I have not done you any harm, fat head. I won't go back. You ought to go there for a fortnight to see how you would like it, you bald-headed old bastard.'*

Mr Lushington: *'For attempting to take your own life, you will have to find one surety of £5 to keep the peace, or, in default, be imprisoned for one month.'*

The defendant was forcibly removed to the cells.

20. *Some prisoners grew tired of proceedings and would entertain themselves.*

Annie Morlay showed scant respect for the law. Having been found not guilty of drowning her child in a pond, she had been immediately re-arrested for stealing a £50 note and £2 cash. After damning evidence from the clerk at the Bank of England who remembered Annie cashing the bill, the prisoner began to disrupt proceedings at Greenwich Police Court by keeping up a running commentary on the evidence: at other times she would hum or whistle tunes. Annie insisted she would not waste her breath in questioning the witness and accused some of the court officials of going to sleep. When Mr Balguy committed her for trial at the Old Bailey she jumped from the dock and did a brisk jig on the courtroom floor.

CAIN NOT ABLE

The most notorious drunkard and perpetual offender found in the East End courts in late Victorian London was Margaret Cain, convicted in the Thames Court over 230 times.

She waited again in the cells in 1889, in 'a deplorable state', making quite a racket, as usual, before being placed in the dock. Once there Margaret started dancing and questioned the magistrate.

'It's fifteen months since I saw you. How are you going on?'

Margaret was charged with being drunk and disorderly, lying on the pavement at Tower Hill, shouting and using filthy language. After hearing the evidence, the magistrate commented that Margaret should be detained in a lunatic asylum.

'I have just come out of one. They could not keep me there',

Margaret proudly informed the court. She followed with,

'Are you the magistrate to give a sentence? What is it to do with you? I've only been here once in fifteen months'.

Mr Saunders sentenced Margaret to fourteen days hard labour, she was removed from the court cursing and swearing. The following report appeared in the East London Advertiser a few months later.

'On Monday, Mr Saunders stated that information had been given him of the death of Margaret Cain, who had been charged at this court several hundreds of times for being drunk, disorderly and assaulting the police. She was the second most notorious character, Bill Onions, now reformed, being the first. It appears that the unhappy woman died in a cell after a violent outburst while under the influence of alcohol.'

Jane Cakebread was after Margaret's record. By 1890, at the age of sixty years and having spent most of her life in prison, she was charged with being drunk and disorderly for the 221st time. She was discovered just after midnight using very bad language to a mob that had surrounded her, and then tried to bite a policeman who endeavoured to break up the gathering. Jane conducted her defence in her usual plausible style:

Prisoner: *'I am very weak and not used to liquor. I had half a quartern of rum and some beer. I am exceedingly sorry and will return you many thanks if you will let me go. When I was in the cell singing my hymns* (Laughter) *the inspector let the police come in and bang me about. I like the police and dote the ground they walk upon* (Laughter) *but not when they knock me about. I have always been a thorough hardworking person, a parlour-maid single-handed* (Laughter) *but am now very weak and will return you thanks if you let me go . . .'*

Ms Cakebread was given the choice of being fined 40s. or imprisoned for one month. She took the familiar path to the cells.

21. *Scenes from Farmfield reformatory for female inebriates sent from the capital.*

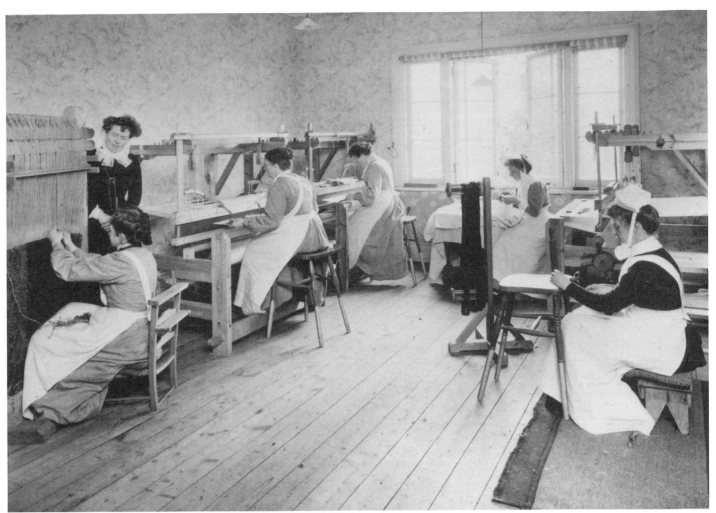

22. *Opened in Surrey in 1900, the maximum sentence on the 'farm' was three years.*

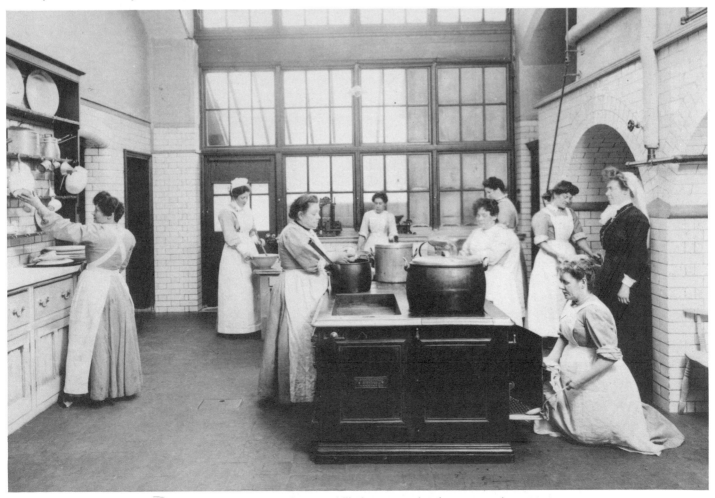

23. *One of the first experiments in trying to teach new skills in a completely new environment.*

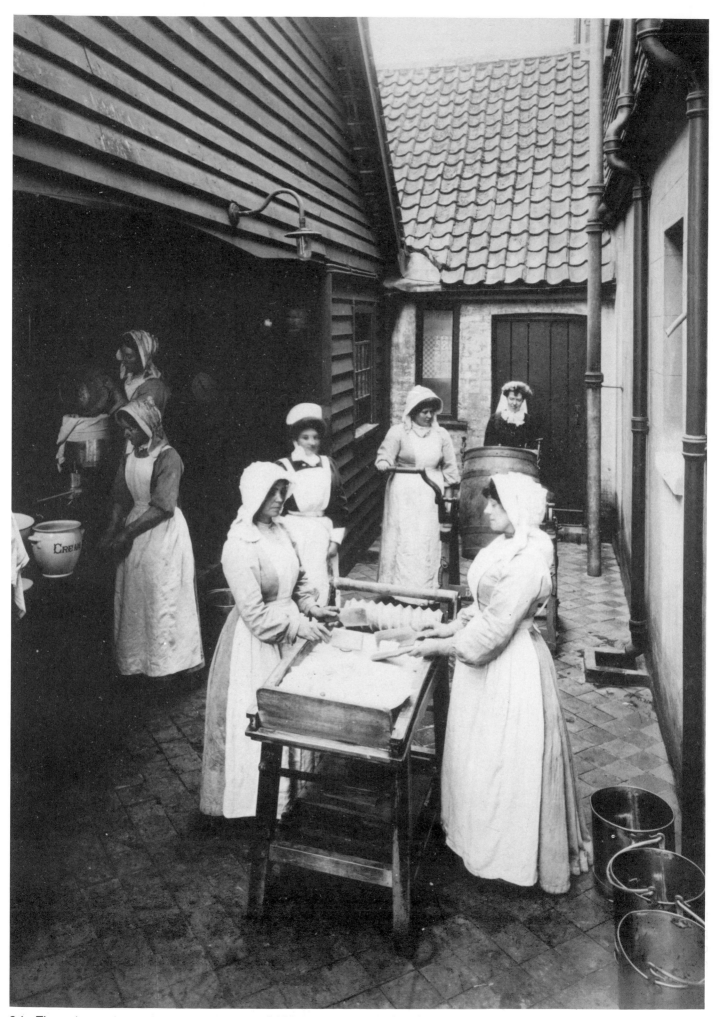

24. *The scheme was not a great success. of 109 women returned to the community in 1909 sixty relapsed almost immediately.*

JENNY DIVER, QUEEN OF THE MOLL BUZZERS

Mary Young was an ambitious and intelligent young Irish girl, proficient in reading, writing and needlework. Not only did she possess academic skills she was also a good mixer and by the age of fifteen had received a proposal of marriage from one of the besotted local young men. Attracted by the exciting stories she had heard of London town Mary consented, provided her would-be husband took her to the capital.

Here she sought out one of her countrywomen, Anne Murphy, and they shared lodgings, with Mary endeavouring to earn an honest living with her needle. Very soon she fell on hard times, the inability to make ends meet by lawful means made her vulnerable to the suggestions of her friend Anne. Vowing her to secrecy, the older woman took Mary to a kind of club where she first made acquaintance with the sort of people with whom she would mix for the rest of her life: pickpockets, footpads and burglars. The first group introduced to Mary specialised in cutting off women's pockets and stealing watches from men near the theatres. Mary lived as man and wife with one of her tutors, taking her studies seriously whilst preparing herself for her first dive. There were great expectations as Mary was considered a very capable student. In fact she exceeded all these expectations by removing a diamond ring after shaking hands with the victim, he not noticing the loss until some time later. Indeed Mary was so proficient at her new job that her friends nicknamed her Jenny Diver and as such we shall continue the story of her extraordinary life.

Jenny was an innovative and extremely cunning criminal. Her next crime involved the use of an artificial set of arms and hands which she tied about herself, her real arms being concealed under her clothes. Filling her stays to appear pregnant, Jenny set off for church in a sedan chair. Meeting the approval of the two elderly ladies on either side, Jenny seemed to be worshiping with great devotion. As they stood to leave Jenny managed to steal both their watches, passing them on to an accomplice in an adjoining pew. As the congregation prepared to depart, the loss was discovered. One of the women complained that the watch must have been taken either by the devil or the pregnant woman—to which the other replied that she could vindicate the pregnant lady whose hands she was sure had not been removed from her lap during the whole time of her being in the pew.

Jenny adjourned to a public house and removed her false arms and 'baby', and was back in church that very evening this time stealing a gentleman's gold watch without being detected.

With her forceful personality and expertise at dipping, Jenny was greatly admired by the rest of the gang and became the mastermind behind a new series of offences.

The young Irish woman had a very fertile imagination with the next robbery taking place in the East End. Her lover, in the guise of a footman, knocked at the door of a prosperous looking house and asked that his mistress could be admitted for a few minutes, as she was taken seriously ill. Because of their smart appearance, the female householder allowed them inside and whilst they were downstairs looking for medicines to help the poor woman, she was going through their drawers, quickly concealing sixty guineas about her person. Her 'footman' was not idle either, pocketing six silver tablespoons, a

pepper box and a salt cellar from the kitchen. Even as the householder was holding a smelling bottle under Jenny's nose to try to clear her head, the young woman was picking her pocket of her purse. The impudence did not stop here, as, when she left, Jenny invited the trusting lady to have tea at her house at a later date!

Pretty Jenny did like to diversify. Hiring lodgings in Covent Garden, the ever inventive moll-buzzer put on her most expensive finery in preparation for a carefully laid plan. She was to attend the theatre, when the King was present, to try and catch the attention of any rich and gullible young men up from the country. In short, she was intent upon 'clocking the countryman' and her prey was a young gentleman of fortune from Yorkshire. This man was not backward about coming forward and whispering to Jenny that she had made a conquest, they returned to 'her place' where he was expecting to get a little supper. He was disappointed as Jenny informed him that she was newly married but agreed to receive him at a future date, when her husband was out.

The prey returned a few days later, sporting a gold-headed cane, a sword with a gold hilt, a gold watch and a diamond ring. He was met by two of Jenny's accomplices dressed as footmen, and her friend, Anne Murphy, acting as waiting-maid. The presence of brothel creeps was fairly well-known so Jenny had to be a little more imaginative. Within minutes the Yorkshireman had removed his ring and then his clothes, when there was an urgent tapping on the door. The 'lady's-maid' whispered that the master of the house had unexpectedly returned. Jenny insisted that the gentleman covered himself with the bedclothes and she would take his apparel into another room to hide. Informing him that she would persuade her husband to sleep in another room and return to his arms as soon as possible, Jenny left. With morning came the realisation that all was not as his young lady friend had suggested. The gull rang the bell and the other people from the house were confronted with a locked door housing a very vexed visitor. The young man sent for some money and clothes and left the establishment poorer to the tune of over one hundred guineas.

Jenny always returned to her favoured form of theft but luck ran out and she was sentenced to transportation for pickpocketing and imprisoned in Newgate for four months to await her passage. During this time she managed to assemble a great deal of property, bought with her ill-gotten gains, and arrived in Virginia a fairly rich and well-respected woman. Jenny did not take to life in the colonies and using her undoubted charms persuaded a young man to take her on board a ship leaving for England. Upon arrival she immediately stole all the possesions she could carry and eventually made her way back to London. Bloke-buzzing was in her blood, Jenny was finally apprehended on London Bridge—she gave her name as Jane Webb—as anybody returning from transportation could expect the death sentence.

Once again Jenny was transported and was back again within twelve months.

Knowing no life other than theft, Jenny was recaptured and this time sentenced to death. Whilst awaiting her execution, Jenny found God and became a devout christian, and insisted that her three-year-old son should be carefully instructed in the teachings of the Bible. On the 18th March, 1740, Jenny was hanged and her body buried in St. Pancras churchyard.

SKINNING

Women were involved in all manner of crimes, from picking pockets to highway robbery. The criminal mind is extremely inventive and very little was safe from the fertile imagination of Victorian thieves, not even the shirt on your back. Skinning would usually take place in winter and was nearly always an offence perpetrated by women. They would entice well-clad children into some dark alleyway or corner and strip the frightened tots of their clothes and boots. This crime was particulary popular with older women, not requiring a great deal of strength or speed.

In 1850 'a showily dressed young woman of thirty' was brought before a magistrate on a charge of 'skinning'. The court was heaving with little boys and girls, all claiming to have been stripped by Susan Nunn. She was picked out by many in an identification parade and sent for trial at the Old Bailey.

Not only children were robbed of their clothes. John Murray had worked at the Tower for thirty years. The last thing he expected returning home one evening was that he would be stripped by two women. They even went as far as removing his silk stockings and gold ring.

John told the court that he had been picked up by the prisoner in the dock and another woman who had invited him back to a house. He declined the offer but was then pushed,

'they stripped me naked. . .After they had taken my clothes, they all ran away.'

Sarah Birk was in the dock and obviously held her victim in contempt, as she had told her friend;

'I stripped a man stark naked and sold his clothes . . . a good middling working man, but a foolish son of a b . . . . .'

SHOPLIFTING AND SECRETING

One of the niches women carved out for themselves in the criminal world was that of hiding stolen goods either on the street or in their houses.

Young thieves received only a fraction of the value of their ill-gotten gains, having to pass them on quickly to a 'fence', who would make good use of every part of her body and home to secrete the booty. A woman whose pitch was in Whitechapel put handkerchiefs and similar items down her bosom, and hid bacon, bread and cheese about her barrow in secret places.

Accomplices in shoplifting adopted the following strategy:

'They will open a piece of stuff and hold it up between the owner and their partner that sits down with her petticoats half up, ready for the word nap it; then she puts it between her carriers (that is a cant word for thighs) and then gets up and lets her cloaths drop . . . and so walks off.'

One of the most notorious of fences in the early nineteenth century was Mrs Jennings of Red Lion Market, where she kept a house of ill-repute.

'She has secret rooms by doors out of cupboards where she plants or secretes the property she buys till she has got it disposed of. Innumerable girls and boys of the youngest class resort to this house and she makes up more beds than any other house in that part of the metropolis; each room in her house (which is a large one) being divided into various divisions for beds and the house is thronged every night. She sanctions robberies in her house which are continually committed by the girls on strangers who they can inveigle into the house and whom the girls will bilk into the bargain . . .'

Anything and everything had a value to the fence and a Mrs White of Wigmore Street, kept an old shoe shop and bought chiefly brushes, pails and coal scuttles etc., which little boys sneaked from gentlemen's houses.

Mrs Diner of Holborn, was a little more up-market, specialising in silk handkerchiefs which she openly displayed for sale after first removing the owner's marks.

Mother Cummings of St. Giles', was one of the most popular fences paying top prices. She also trained up young criminals and was the keeper of a bawdy-house, offering rooms to customers 'either to sleep there all the night or for what time they please', from 1s. upto 5s. 6d..

Male clients also had to be wary of 'creeps'—brothel thieves who would quietly crawl along the floor to examine the clothes of that 'sucker' who is in bed with a woman.

Men are very vulnerable at the height of passion with their mind on one goal whilst the woman, if she was a 'file and buttock' would be picking the pocket whilst in the act of coition. Something else to think about rather than worrying that the ceiling needs painting.

THE HOMESICK KIWI

Harriet was desperate to return to her father in New Zealand. Work in the London of 1889 had been difficult to find and, after a few sessions as an artist's model, the tall, attractive, well-dressed young woman thought of an ingenious scheme to make her way home. This plan led her to be standing in the dock, charged with stealing; a coat, tie, hat, boots and overcoat, value £3 10s., the property of Mr George Johnson, a musician from Battersea. George told his story to the court as Harriet, who had her hair closely cropped, listened attentively.

On Monday night between eleven and twelve, whilst walking in Victoria Street, Westminster, the musician met the prisoner casually, and entered into a conversation with her. They had refreshments, and afterwards, at her invitation, went back to her lodgings. He remembered drinking a glass of ale but could recall nothing else until the following morning, when he discovered, to his great surprise, that his clothes, hat and boots had gone. The young lady's clothes had been left but George protested, to the amusement of the court, that they were no use to him.

The landlady had been astonished to hear a male voice coming from Harriet's room and upon investigating, discovered the hapless George who explained that he had nothing left but a flannel shirt.

Harriet had deliberately chosen somebody of her own size so the clothes would fit, and early next morning tried to enlist as a male steward on board a boat due to sail to New Zealand. When rejected for not being able to provide a reference, the former chorus girl who had played in 'Puss in Boots', tried to enlist. She had not been aware that there were formalities for recruits if one wanted to trade one pair of boots for another. Harriet asserted that she would have returned the clothes at a later date, but when police arrested her at St. James's Workhouse, in male attire, she was completely broke. The magistrate displayed a fairly lenient attitude, saying he was going to think over the case to see if he could find a way of getting the young lady in men's clothes, back to New Zealand.

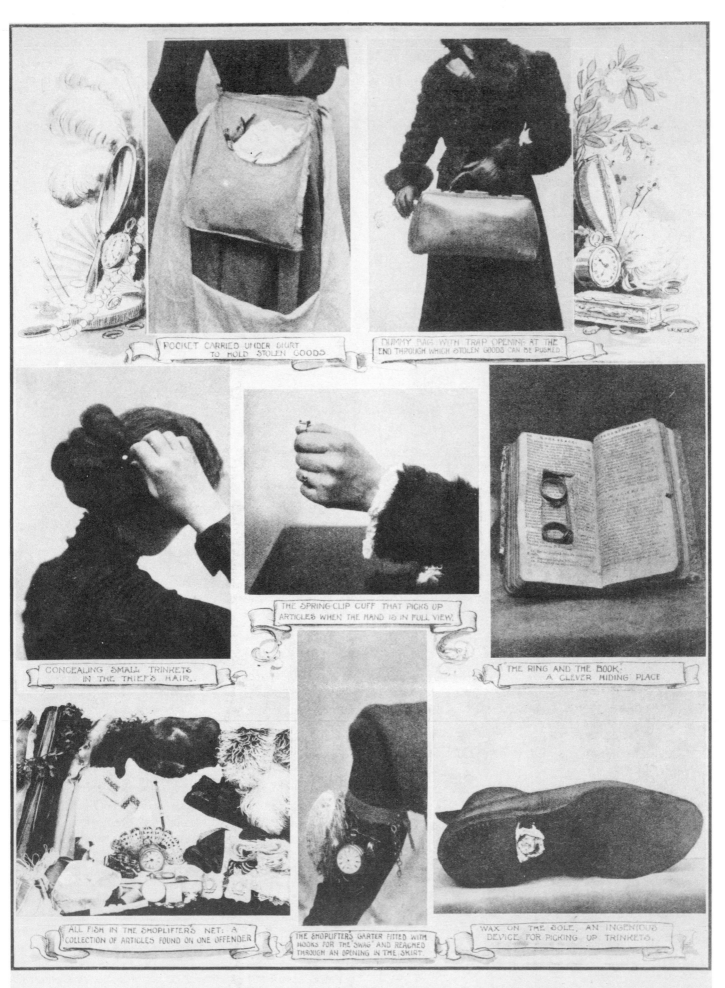

POCKET CARRIED UNDER SKIRT TO HOLD STOLEN GOODS

DUMMY BAG WITH TRAP OPENING AT THE END THROUGH WHICH STOLEN GOODS CAN BE PUSHED

THE SPRING CLIP CUFF THAT PICKS UP ARTICLES WHEN THE HAND IS IN FULL VIEW.

CONCEALING SMALL TRINKETS IN THE THIEF'S HAIR.

THE RING AND THE BOOK: A CLEVER HIDING PLACE

ALL FISH IN THE SHOPLIFTER'S NET: A COLLECTION OF ARTICLES FOUND ON ONE OFFENDER

THE SHOPLIFTER'S GARTER FITTED WITH HOOKS FOR THE SWAG AND REACHED THROUGH AN OPENING IN THE SKIRT.

WAX ON THE SOLE, AN INGENIOUS DEVICE FOR PICKING UP TRINKETS.

SHOP-LIFTING MADE EASY: THE INGENIOUS DEVICES OF WOMAN THIEVES.

Very few people would guess that shop-lifting has been made an exact science, and that its mere machinery constitutes a formidable museum. How successful the art may be in expert hands is proved by the really extraordinary haul discovered on the person of one woman, and here photographed.

25. Shop-lifting. A crime as old as shops themselves.

JUVENILE CRIME

Parents and guardians at their wits end would often go to the courts to ask advice as to how to change the behaviour of their charges. One grandmother brought to court the 5½ year old boy who was making her life a misery: the magistrate saw the problem at first hand as the young man critically examined whatever lay near him and then went walkabout in the courtroom wandering upto the bench and installing himself for the hearing.

The lad just loved riding in cabs and trams. Instead of going to school he would call a cabman from the rank, inform him that he was wanted in a distant street and then get in for the ride. On Monday of that week in 1890, he took a tram-car to Kentish-Town and returned home in a cab. The grandmother was besieged everyday by cabmen demanding fares. Because of his age there was very little advice the magistrate could offer other than recommending the truancy board if he persisted in refusing to attend school.

SENDING A BOY TO SCHOOL MANACLED

26. *One surefire way of preventing truancy.*

Drastic steps were sometimes taken by desperate parents when their children openly disobeyed them. One such boy refused to return home after school, preferring to stay out all night. His parents came up with a novel solution to the problem, sending him to his (Dartford) school with a large chain and padlock tied to his ankles. When asked by the headteacher to remove the restraints the mother would not. To avoid uproar in the classroom he was refused entry.

BOYS WILL BE YOBS

A case before Mr Balguy in Woolwich, 1883 would not look out of place in one of today's courts. The offender was a 15-year-old boy charged with stealing a piece of wood, valued 6d.

Frank White was caught red-handed, spotted by a police constable leaving the woodyard with a plank in his hand and one between his ears. The predictable excuse was put forward, that Frank had found the wood in the grass. His mother supported the defence by stating that her son was a good boy (well, she would, wouldn't she) and that he only took the wood to play with.

Mr Balguy had great experience of these types of cases and apparently little patience with these types of offenders.

Mr Balguy: *'I think the boys about Woolwich are most unbearable and yet their mothers come before me and tell me they are angels.'*

The magistrate seemed the better judge of character when it was later revealed that the boy had previously been convicted for stealing cigars and a clock. The prisoner, along with his companions, was causing the local police a lot of headaches.

The magistrate had obviously had his fill of young offenders, indicating that he would like to abolish all boys from Woolwich, he went on to say:

'I never met with such an incorrigible set of boys as there are about Woolwich. They will let nothing alone. They will not even let their fathers or anyone else grow or have anything. It is always necessary to have a brick in one hand to be able to administer it when required.'

When it was suggested that the boy might profit from a spell on a training ship, Mr Balguy replied:

'Why, if I had a training ship just outside the door here, I would be able to fill it in less than five minutes.'

Frank White was fined 10s. or seven days imprisonment.

On other occasions Mr Balguy recommended the birch. A fourteen-year-old and twelve-year-old were sentenced to twelve strokes and six strokes respectively, for stealing two bottles of sweets, and another boy six strokes, for stealing a bottle of lemonade, value 2d.

At the start of the nineteenth century boys as young as seven years old were considered responsible for their actions, and therefore liable to the full imposition of the law. William Crawford visited over eight hundred young thieves, mostly in prisons, and submitted a report on juvenile delinquecy in the metropolis. Detailed below are two typical delinquency records on young offenders:

A.B. aged thirteen years. His parents are living; he was but for a short time at school; his father was frequently intoxicated, and on these occasions the son generally left home, and associated with bad characters, who introduced him to houses of ill-fame, where they gambled till they had lost or spent all their money. This boy had been five years in the commission of crime, and had been imprisoned for three separate offences; sentence of death had been twice passed on him.

27. *The cameraman was on hand to record this dramatic chase involving a policeman and young thief on Blackheath.*

28. *"O.K. It's a fair cop. I'll come quietly."*

E.F. aged eight years. His mother only is living, and she is of a very immoral character. This boy has been in the habit of stealing for upwards of two years. In Covent-Garden Market there is a party of between thirty and forty boys who sleep every night under the shed and baskets . . . this child was one of the number; and it appears that he has been brought up to the several police offices under eighteen separate charges. He has twice been confined in the House of Correction, and three times in Bridewell; he is very ignorant, but of a good capacity.

A random selection from the prisoners detained at Coldbath Fields in 1833 is further evidence of the harsh penalties meted out to young offenders. Prison number 250, Andrew McCarth, 8, was sentenced to two months hard labour, solitary confinement and two whippings for petty theft. Prisoners 393 and 472, nine and eight years old respectively, both received three calendar months for being a 'rogue and vagabond'.

Thomas Evans, at 15, had been sentenced to death for a felony, but this had later been changed to one year's hard labour, two month's solitary confinement to be followed by transporation for life.

It was a point of honour to take punishment 'like a man', showing contempt for authority. Some of the lads did not fear transportation despite the horrific stories they surely heard about conditions in the boats.

Thoughts of adventure in distant lands helped allay the fears of the journey and they were leaving very little behind. If young boys had to pay the ultimate sacrifice for their crimes they would try to 'die game' going to the gallows in some stolen finery and showing contempt for all the proceedings in front of their friends who knew their turn might come at any time.

29. Boys as young as eight might be sentenced to death for minor theft.

The Dreadful Life and
Confession of a Boy, Aged Twelve Years

Who was Condemn'd to Die at the last Old Bailey Sessions.

WITH horror we attempt to relate the progress of evil, generally prevailing among children, through the corrupt example of wicked parents; though we are constrained to confess that many a child through bad company, wickedly follow the dictates of their own will, and often bring the hoary heads of honest parents with sorrow to the grave. The horrors of a guilty conscience crieth to heaven for vengeance against such wretched parents as belonged to T. King, who after eloping from their native place, took obscure lodgings in East Smithfield, where they harboured the vilest characters, & wickedly encouraged the only son in lying, stealing, &c. At the age of 7 years the parish humanely bound him an apprentice but his wickedness soon caused his master to discharge him.—He was afterwards bound to a chimney-sweeper in the Borough, who soon repented having taken him, for he plundered every place that he was sent to work at, for which not only correction but imprisonment ensued. His master being an honest man, brought him twice back with some property he had stolen which obtained him pardon, and prevented him from being transported.

Lastly, his parents made him desert from his master, and bound him to a gang of theives who sent him down the chimney of a jeweller in Swallow-st., where he artfully unbolted the shop window, out of which his companions cut a pane of glass, and he handed a considerable quantity of articles to them; but the noise he made alarmed the family, and he was taken into custody, but the others escaped.

He was tried at the last Old Bailey Sessions, found Guilty, and sentenced to die in the 12th year of his age. After his sentence the confession he made struck those around him with horror, stating the particulars of several murders and robberies. We hope the dreadful example of this wretched youth may produce a lasting warning to the world at large.

MISERABLE BEGGARS

The squalor of life on the streets and in the workhouse

30. *A blind beggar, around 1900. Many had regular haunts they would frequent for years.*

Because of the large numbers of Londoners on the breadline in Victorian days, to make a living as a beggar one had to appear even more deprived and wasted than the average under-nourished worker. Ingenious methods were employed to prise pennies from the caring members of society.

Some beggars, by bandaging a lump of raw meat to one of their limbs, made it resemble an open wound. Others would cover a patch of skin with a layer of soap and then add strong vinegar creating an impression of large, yellow blisters. Even beggars with unfeigned mutilations would make the most of their misfortune by touching up the stumps of amputations so they might seem raw and painful.

A clotted, dirty bandage might be applied to the eye or ear, with the beggar slowly revealing the supposed injury, banking on the fact that few would want to stay more than a very short time in his presence. Other beggars might 'work the shallow' that is shivering or shaking violently in cold weather while wearing very little. Sometimes these beggars were donated cast-offs which they would sell to stall holders, there being a large market for second-hand

clothes. The one thing all these beggars depended upon was that their appearance would revolt the public so much that they would donate a few coppers and move on as quickly as possible to escape the distressing spectacles confronting them.

Others had a different modus operandi. A beggar might be seen with a card detailing his sad life-story slung around his neck. Genuine blind beggars and sham blind beggars would use dogs taught to stop when any prosperous looking passer-by was encountered. One, however, complained that his dog had not been properly trained as he would often stop to 'have a word' with another dog, leaving his owner to relate a pathetic tale to just the two canines, who probably had other things on their minds.

Some optimistic beggars must have banked on their prey being almost blind. After the publication of 'Uncle Tom's Cabin' there was a speight of negro slaves found begging on the streets of the capital. A closer examination of these slaves would have discovered white bodies and limbs—the blackened face being about as convincing as a black and white minstrel.

If adults were poor beggars themselves, they could often live on the earnings of children. The following account is taken from 'The Pauper, the Thief and the Convict' by Thomas Archer.

'Standing by the terminus of the North London Railway, for instance, you may witness the periodical visits of slinking and bedraggled women—weedy as to their apparel, and with the attenuation and pallid hue of much gin on their faces—who come to take off one or other of these poor little wretches the money they have 'picked up' during the day. Any one of these women may be the mother of one or more of the children, or may merely employ them to do her cadging. Sometimes she brings them slices of coarse bread and butter wrapped in a dingy handkerchief; occasionally a heavy-eyed sodden looking man will wait for her at the street corner, or, in her absence, may himself secure the few coppers which he extorts from the child, with an anxious glance round him lest he be observed. Both he and the woman, should they catch the eye of a passenger during their operations, will assume an expression of demure, poverty-stricken resignation, and affect to wipe away a tear as they contrive to display, by well-affected accident, the bread and butter they have 'gone without themselves.'

31. *Probably the most famous photograph of a beggar, taken in the capital around 1870.*

Children could be hired for a few pence a day or permanently transferred for a few shillings, and after schooling would be put on the streets to support their new owners.

To be alive without means of support was a criminal offence, although most police simply had to turn a blind eye to the vast numbers of beggars on the streets—many of whom had genuine hard-luck stories and disabilities. In Colbath Fields House of Correction in the 1850's less than one per cent of the prisoners were held for 'begging or sleeping in open air'.

32. *Having lost his complaint the blind man was forced to move on.*

One blind man complained of harrassment by the police in 1887. For years he had stood in the same place on the King's Road, Chelsea. The dog sat beside him with a can fastened around its neck, into which coins might be dropped. When a man teased the dog by pretending to drop a coin in the can, the normally docile, well-behaved animal went for the joker and bit his hand. The blind man was told that he would have to get rid of his dog and the appeal fell on deaf ears as the magistrate supported the police action.

Continuing the canine theme one of the best known beggars in Holborn was 'The Barker.' This youngish woman had three means of 'earning' her daily bread. When not collecting orange and lemon skins to be sold to distillers, she would pad herself up to feign pregnancy and gain sympathy from the passing crowds. Her most famous trick, however, was to pretend to be suffering a fit, howling and barking like a dog, taking to her heels when the police arrived.

One of the fastest runners in the East End was a beggar who supposedly had a wooden leg, but when challenged by a constable would invariably sprint off and lose himself in a crowd.

One of the many cases of children being brought to court for begging is taken from the East London Advertiser, under the headline 'A Baby Beggar'.

'Michael Cain, aged six, who was too small to be placed in the dock, and who was stood on the seat in front of the

33. *Dinner at Marylebone Workhouse, 1900.*

solicitors' table, was charged with begging—Constable 49 H.R. said he saw the lad begging from the foot passengers in the Commercial Road on Saturday afternoon. He had no shoes on and appeared to be almost perished through cold and exposure. The child said his mother sent him out begging every day and if he did not take home more than 10d. she gave him a beating—the mother was called, and said her husband was in the infirmary. She denied having sent him out to beg. He always had plenty to eat. Mr Saunders allowed the boy to go away with his mother.'

Many beggars alternated between the streets and the workhouse.

WORKHOUSE CRIME

What punishment was open to supervisors of a workhouse when able-bodied paupers refused to work? Could one sink any lower? John Cole, a 19-year-old was brought before the magistrates in 1889 for neglecting to perform his allotted task of work. After not completing his job on the Friday, Cole was put on rations of bread and water for the following 48 hours. He then bluntly refused to do any work at all and was therefore handed in to custody. After being told by Cole that he could not work on bread and water, the magistrate showed him a great deal of sympathy, saying that workhouse officials should not have the power to sentence workers to these rations. He was ordered to serve one day in prison where he probably received a better diet.

Another sympathetic hearing was given to a self-styled workhouse lawyer. He was an educated man who repeatedly discharged himself from the workhouse and then had himself re-admitted. When returning he would always arrive in a cab smoking a cigar. He was looked up to as a leader by most of the paupers and one day enticed twenty to accompany him to the committee rooms, each carrying his daily ration of broth. Here the 'lawyer' stated that the broth was not fit for a dog to eat. Several members of the committee then tasted it and pronounced it delicious.

The magistrates found there were no charges to answer and they were all dropped.

Most disputes in the workhouse were feuds between paupers, who, not surprisingly, being in such close proximity, tended to get on each others nerves. In Poplar Workhouse John Stevens was charged with assaulting Francis Wilson. The latter was woken from his sleep by a fist in the face. Still semi-conscious, he was struck again in the eye, blackening it. When Stevens was asked his side of the story he answered:

'Well, he kept snoring and wouldn't leave off, so I just gave him a tap.'

He was sentenced to seven days hard labour.

Despite being forbidden, Emily Phillips was determined to get some boiling water to make tea. When Miss Edith Watts, the task-mistress, of the Fulham Road workhouse, remonstrated with her, the troublesome thirty-two-year-old pauper inmate threatened her life. Seizing the official by the throat, Emily broke a necklace and let forth a torrent of abuse.

Mr Cole was next in line for Emily's verbal tirade as she kicked and tried to bite the master. Her tantrums continued with the breaking of panes of glass before she was restrained.

In court a history of similar offences was read out, the prisoner exhibiting a 'most hardened demeanour', wishing the master to 'drop dead in the witness box'.

Emily's main complaint was about the food, stating that she, along with other able-bodied paupers, had to eat 'black beetle soup', poisonous food and water gruel. She went on to level complaints at the officers who threatened to have her sent to prison. The magistrate had very little time for these grudges, and, after telling her she was living on charity, sentenced the hardened pauper to three months imprisonment, with two months hard labour.

35. St. Martin's workhouse early in the nineteenth century.

Emily might well have made friends with Honora Lucas, just one year older than herself who was sentenced to two weeks hard labour for a similar offence at Marylebone Workhouse. Honora had been admitted with her baby at 9 p.m. after a bout of drinking. She created a rumpus when using foul language, pulling four paupers out of bed and knocking them about. She finished the evening by pulling a 70-year-old from her bed and getting into it herself. She was described as one of the vilest people in the house and was in and out every week, only being admitted for the sake of her baby.

34. Throwing an old woman out of her workhouse bed.

36. The overcrowding led to many disputes coming before the courts.

40

THE LIGHTER SIDE OF COURT LIFE
Some of the more humorous cases presented before the Victorian magistrates' courts

THE COLOURED COMEDIAN

Magistrates must have welcomed a break from the endless number of cases of assault and theft with most prisoners, although plainly guilty, fabricating stories and alibis and making counter claims. A little light relief crept into the Lambeth court in 1881 with the appearance of the 'coloured comedian'.

Having been arrested on the Wednesday night for annoying people in the street and being drunk, he stood dressed up and his face blackened, a banjo in hand.

Mr Saunders (Magistrate): *'What have you to say, prisoner, about getting drunk?'*

Prisoner: *'Well I don't know, but I did get a drop, I suppose.'*

Mr Saunders: *'You should not go about in such a costume, and get drunk and annoy people.'*

Prisoner: *'The costume, your worship, is a recognised institution of the country,'* (loud laughter).

Mr Saunders: *'Well, if that is so, I must fine you.'*

Prisoner: *'My dear sir, you had better not.'* (renewed laughter).

Mr Saunders: *'I must.'*

Prisoner: *'Well, make it small.'*

Mr Saunders: *'You must pay 5s.'*

Prisoner: *'Now really, my dear sir, you must make it less than that—say half-a-crown.'*

Mr Saunders: *'No 5s..'*

Prisoner: *'Really, my dear sir, you can alter it. Make it half-a-crown.'*

Mr Saunders: (who was amused at the style of the prisoner), *'Well I will make it half-a-crown.'*

The magistrate was immediately thanked in 'most flowery terms' amidst great laughter and the coloured comedian stepped from court.

COOLING HIS BRAINS

Drink often provokes a dangerous desire to swim, even in a river as polluted as the Thames. Charles Regan decided to cool off in the water after soaking his brains with alcohol on the land.

At a quarter to twelve, Police Constable Saward was called to the foreshore where he found the prisoner naked, bathing in front of the whole town. He managed to get some clothes on him before sending for an ambulance. When it arrived, Charles became violent, kicking the policeman's leg. In court the prisoner gave as his reason for bathing that he wished to cool his brains.

Mr Balguy: *'I dare say his brains want cooling pretty often.'*

Prisoner: *'I wasn't naked, I bathed in my shirt.'*

Constable: *'You had only your boots and socks on when I saw you.'*

Prisoner: *'Yes, I took off my shirt to put my trousers on'* (Laughter). *'I was not drunk, your honour. I was only exhausted from the way I was handled by the police.'*

Mr Balguy ordered Charles Regan to be imprisoned for two weeks, claiming that assaulting the police and acting 'very indecently' were serious offences.

FLYING FISH

John protested that the fish he bought was bad. Before the shopkeeper had time to inspect the offending goods, the piece of fish was flying across the shop. The affronted customer was not a skilled thrower and the poor assistant was the recipient of the aforementioned bad fish. There then ensued a general free-for-all when other customers picked up oysters and fried fish and threw them across the shop, breaking the windows and gas fittings. To try and quell the riot, the shop owner and his assistant threw hot fat at the troublemakers, they beating a hasty retreat.

At court John Thery was charged with damaging gas fittings to the value of £5.

The defendant said that the fish he bought was unfit for food. The shop owner refused to change it saying that if the defendant ate it, 'it would do him good'. They was ordered to pay his share of the costs and fined 5s.

'I'LL DANCE ON YOUR GRAVE'

Very few would actually put the threat of dancing on somebody else's grave into practice. One of those few was Matilda Todhunter in 1889.

A police constable was called to Cannon Street road by a woman who said that the 45-year-old Mrs Todhunter was dancing on her (the informant's) husband's corpse. The policeman proceeded to the kitchen where he found the defendant drunkenly dancing on a coffin containing a man's body. He managed to get her down but she jumped back up and pulled off the sheet which covered the body. With great difficulty the drunken woman was removed from the room, but continued her frenzied dancing in the street.

The charge of being drunk and disorderly was denied by the accused. She stated that the corpse had been lying in the house for a fortnight. Matilda Todhunter was sentenced to fourteen days hard labour.

37. *Plumstead High Street showing The Green Man and Red Lion (the author may be found here celebrating after Charlton matches.)*

PLASTERED IN PLUMSTEAD

John Simmonds of Plumstead Common was summoned for trespassing in search of game.

Mr Balguy: *'There, prop him up somewhere'* (Laughter). *'Can you understand what's said?'*

The defendant made no reply.

Mr Balguy: *'Gilham, ask him if he can understand.'*

Sergeant Gilham: (in a stentorian voice) *'The magistrate asks if you can understand?'*

Defendant: (in a whining tone) *'I don't think I can.'* (Loud laughter).

Mr Balguy: *'Nor I either.'*

Defendant: (Crying and wiping his eyes with his sleeve) *'I was drunk when I went there, and I'm drunk now.'* (Laughter).

Mr Balguy: *'Ah, that's the worst stage of drunkenness.'*

DRESSED IN WOMEN'S CLOTHING

One of the theories as to the identity of Jack the Ripper was that he was dressed in ladies' clothing so he might approach his victims without suspicion and flee the scene undetected. It was no surprise therefore in 1889, that a crowd of some six hundred people gathered in the East End when a man wearing women's clothes was apprehended. Word got round that the Ripper had been caught.

At his trial, Edward Hambler was charged with disorderly conduct and being dressed in female attire. The 61-year-old offered no explanation as to why he was so dressed. Inspector Arthur Ferrett was the arresting officer. He was attracted by the cries of a large crowd, two of whom had apprehended the prisoner. He was wearing a woman's hat and veil, now in evidence, a black jacket, print dress and a large dress-improver (Laughter).

The prisoner said that it was only a freak and was bound over in the sum of £10 to keep the peace for three months.

IT'S A WISE WOMAN

Without the sophisticated scientific tests we have today, proving a man to be the father of an illegitimate child in order to receive contributions for its upkeep was a very difficult business. After having the case dismissed twice by London magistrates, a mother tried again in Croydon in 1881. A third rejection was too much for the child's grandmother who held the baby in her arms and shouted out:

'The case was cruelly dismissed! The case was cruelly dismissed'. 'There is good evidence to show who is the father of the child, and that is the young man over there'. (pointing to the defendant).

Warming to her task, the grandmother surveyed the court through her large glasses and then produced her evidence. Taking off the baby's bonnet and holding the young boy at arm's length she caused roars of laughter when claiming:

'That's a young . . . . . ; look at his profile!'

38. *"May I present exhibit one your honour."*

The chairman said that he could do nothing other than dismiss the case. The mother now joined the affray:

'Look at that scamp of a man; I'd like to smash him!'

The outraged grannie had not finished yet:

'I haven't done with him yet! I'll carry the law to the farthest extent, if I spend my last penny!'

The mother now became hysterical at what she knew to be a miscarriage of justice and as she was carried out of court by the police she was comforted by her mother:

'Never mind, my girl, we will make him pay yet.'

The accused's application for costs was turned down.

THE BLACK MAGICIAN

Who hasn't been tempted to find out what joys or miseries the future may hold? For centuries we've been crossing palms with silver and listening to stories of handsome and rich young men or beautiful ladies we are to meet. Not surprisingly, the more silver we part with the rosier our future.

How might these predictions be changed if the fortune-teller were taken to court for being a fraud? The 'Black Magician', alias James Caroll, was charged at Lambeth Street in 1828 with the following offence: 'Defrauding amorous youths, maids, wives and widows of sundry sums of money, under pretence of unravelling to them the mysteries of their approaching fates'.

The first witness to appear was a pretty little brunette, Cecilia Johnson. Having heard marvellous accounts of the Black Magician, she visited his house to see what was to become of her. The future seemed full of promise as there was somewhere a man expiring for love of her; he would marry her, they would produce a large family and live happily ever after.

Sir Daniel Williams: (magistrate), *'Well, Miss, it was no doubt very agreeable; ladies, and young ones especially, wish to hear that young men are dying for them. What did you give him, pray, for this joyous communication?'*

Cecilia: (smiling) *Only threepence your worship.'*

To the general amusement of the court she continued earnestly;

'Ah, sir, there is no young man dying for me; I wish there was: he is an imposter.'

The next witness was described as 'a matronly- looking' female who went to see the 'sable-soothsayer', once again parting with threepence.

Sir Daniel Williams: *'Are you a married woman?'*

Matron: *'Yes, sir.'*

Sir Daniel: *'And have a family . . . then indeed you are a very silly person; there is some excuse for the credulous follies and fancies of young people but you have none.'*

The magistrate dismissed the evidence of 'the matron', but that of a young lad who went to see the Black Magician as a lark, led to his conviction.

The young boy, dressed in his sister's clothes, after handing over his threepence was informed that he was a very pretty girl. The Magician went further stating, that if he were not already married he would select 'her' to be his wife. He must have noticed a gleam in the customer's eye and told his client that 'she' had been imprudent and was some months gone with child! The customer could hold back no longer, exposing himself as a boy and the Black Magician as a fraud.

The prisoner's defence was as follows:

Prisoner: *'Vel, your vorship, you sees as how a number of leddies come to me aboutin deir fortins. I no send for 'em, if de wish to hab their fortins told, I can't helps 'em'.*

Sir Daniel: *'Ah, but you can: What do you say to taking the threepence from each?'*

When the defendant offered no reply his immediate fate, probably unforseen, was a sentence under the Vagrancy Act to 14 days on the treadmill.

39. *Religious zealots would often interrupt church services.*

LEWIS THE LIGHT, ELIAS THE DOG BITE

Magistrates were asked to deal with all manner of cases, some of the most difficult involved religious zealots who interrupted services in extraordinary ways, but appeared and acted in a totally sane manner the rest of the time.

Such a person was Jane Greenslade, an attractive thirty-year-old who stood before the Westminster Police Court. She wore a black cashmir dress with a closely fitting jacket of brown material, her blonde hair contrasted with the velvet bonnet. A green satin ribbon was tied around the hat with the words ''Queen of Hades', clearly visible. Jane calmly waited for the proceedings to begin.

On the preceding Sunday in Brompton Oratory, just as the sermon was about to begin, Jane had leapt from her pew and taking a bundle of handbills from her pocket, she threw them into the air, scattering them amongst the congregation. The bills, two of which are quoted below, were handed up to the magistrate.

'Asinine dunces, heathen Christians, ignorant infidels, simple zanies-All Stay in Hell and be damned:—All. Act! Words are useless, meaningless; You have talked yourself deaf, blind, mad, dead. You have traduced and prostituted all deeds and words, even my words and works, until the vilest depravity is regarded as the greatest good, and Truth himself is made an Infernal Liar Elias the 2 edged sword. The Great Teacher, Alpha and Omega, Lewis the Light'.

A second more unintelligible leaflet was signed, Lewis the Light, Elias the Dog Bite, 'See the conquering hero comes' Ha! Ha!! Ha!!!

'Lewis the Light' who had signed both leaflets had passed through the courts three weeks previously. He had

been remanded in a lunatic asylum and subsequently released. Rumour went round that he was in court to witness his wife's trial, for it was indeed his wife and mother of his children who stood in the dock. Nobody, however, could see 'The Light'.

More evidence was heard against Jane.

'The prisoner took a crucifix out of her pocket and dashed it violently to the ground, breaking the image to pieces.'

After the prisoner had been forcibly ejected, she tried to get back into the building and a constable was sent for.

Jane stood in a perfectly composed manner throughout the testimony and when asked if she would like to question the witnesses, declined in a meek tone. The assistant clerk then asked Jane where she had been these last few days. She seemed not to know nor care, changing her story twice. The three children had been admitted to the workhouse.

Mr D'Eyncourt now started questioning the prisoner directly.

Mr D'Eyncourt: *'What have you to say to the disturbed congregation?'*

Prisoner: (in a low tone) *'I am only half here. I am only responsible to my husband and to nobody else. I deny that I broke any laws . . . I have nothing to say, I am not responsible to anyone but my husband.'*

Upon being remanded for a week in Holloway so that medical men could comment on the state of her mind, Jane merely smiled and bowed to the magistrate, she seemed to have an inner glow. She must have seen 'The Light'.

'A LUNATIC NOT UNDER PROPER CONTROL'

Many prisoners appearing before the magistrates had almost lost their sanity through overindulgence of alcohol. Others were in need of psychological help. Although the magistrates often recognised the problems there was very little in the way of rehabilitation and being 'a lunatic not under proper control' was an offence.

In 1899, William Nelson, 21 years of age, was charged with being a wandering lunatic. After spending the whole day touring London in a cab, William refused to pay his fare and the police were called to the West India Road so the cabman might receive his £2. When asked why he had not paid, the defendant replied:

'I met with an accident when I was seven years old: While I was ill I read the life of Nelson. I mean to place myself before the world and doing a great deed, and the papers will be full of it tomorrow. I am worth £70,000.'

William was arrested and taken to the police station where he said he was going to give a banquet at which all the crowned heads of Europe would be present. He went on to invite the inspector and all the constables, saying he would supply each of them with a nice tall silk hat costing 12s. 6d.

In court, William invited the magistrate to attend a banquet with the Queen and once again offered to buy him a nice silk hat. There was no choice but to communicate with one of the primitive asylums and have William locked up. I could find no details of the banquet.

WEEPING OVER HIS RABBITS

One of the ways of ridding oneself of an unwanted partner, eccentric relation or obstructive business colleague, without resorting to murder, was to have the 'offending' person confined to an asylum .

Being mostly privately run, and therefore seeking new business, asylums were not too concerned about the mental state of the patient, more with the healthy state of his or her bank balance. A few examples of cases where friends and relations were seeking to have their loved ones committed—for their own sake of course—reveal more about the state of mind of the doctors than they do of the intended victim.

Edward Davies' mother felt she had to protect her son when he showed signs of rebelling against her domination. On his mother's instructions the tea dealer was committed to a Clapham retreat and several doctors sought out to testify as to his insanity before a tribunal. The 'evidence' against Davies was as follows.

He gave important papers to a person he hardly knew. There was insanity in the family i.e. his paternal uncles. He had learnt to box. He would weep over his little rabbits, which he had not seen for six weeks.

The doctor claimed that Davies was insane 'on the seventh of December because he would not admit to having been insane on the eighth of August'.

Further charges related to Davies being incapable of running his own business, but when questioned the doctor admitted he knew nothing of how he ran his business. He was also accused of making a poor purchase of a country estate, 'considering the circumstances'. When questioned as to the circumstances, the doctor replied he knew 'nothing of Davies' circumstances'.

Probably the best testimony to Edward Davies' insanity, according to the doctor, was that he believed that 'men of honour', such as himself, had an interest in saying what they knew to be untrue.

There was some sanity at the hearing. The jury stopped the case without even hearing any of Davies' witnesses and found in his favour to 'loud and general applause'.

PROPOSAL TO A HOUSEMAID

In a case against a Mr Campbell, one of his symptoms of insanity was his dislike of woollen trousers, he preferring corduroy as they were better for walking.

The Reverend Edward Frank was found to be deranged because he refused to sleep with his wife, allowing another man to take his place whilst he himself committed adultery.

A Mr J. Taylor, a gentleman in his eighties, was accused of being a lunatic chiefly because he asked several women to marry him. Let's hear some of the 'evidence' presented before the commission:

Mr Winslow: *'Don't you think you are rather an old gentleman to think of marrying?'*

Mr Taylor: *'I don't know. Suppose I was 999, what has that got to do with it? I suppose next you will ask me how many hairs I have got on my eyebrows . . .'*

Mr Winslow: *'. . . do you sleep well at night?'*

Mr Taylor: *'I did not sleep well last night.'*

Mr Winslow: *'What do you do when you lie awake?'*

Mr Taylor: *'Oh, I can't tell you that. What do you do? Where do you live? What do you do when you lie awake? My turn is come now; let us have fair play.'* (much laughter).

Mr Winslow: *'You shall have your turn bye-and-bye; now do you sing at night?'*

Mr Taylor: *'Yes, sometimes; I believe there is no act of parliament against singing . . .'*

Mr Winslow: *'But you sing at night!'*

Mr Taylor: *'So do the nightingales.'*

Not surprisingly Mr Taylor complained, 'This is all nonsense, it is an affront to the commission of gentlemen here.'

A verdict of insanity was returned.

The Reverend Leach's family called in the doctor after the clergyman asked his housemaid if she would become his wife. The doctor was convinced that Leach had become unhinged because of his attitude to servants, the Reverend arguing that they ought to be treated more as equals.

'. . . he dined and took his meals with his servants and kissed them in the morning, and allowed them to sit on his knee. He had also said that after family prayers he had his servants in the drawing room and played cards with them until 3.00 in the morning, and between deals he read chapters out of the Bible to them . . .'

Leach was declared sane, though one has to wonder about the doctor.

BEFORE PENAL SERVITUDE
The stocks, pillory, branding, branks and other punishments

40. *A woman exhibited in a cage on London Bridge, probably for some sexual misdemeanour.*

CAPITAL OFFENCES

In 1765 the judge was ordered to pronounce the death sentence for the following offences;
Murder; treason; coining money; arson; rape; sodomy; piracy; forgery; destroying ships or setting them on fire; bankrupts not answering or concealing their effects; burglary; highway robbery; house-breaking; privately stealing or picking pockets above 1s.; shoplifting above 5s.; stealing bonds, bills, or bills from letters; stealing above 40s. in any house; stealing above 40s. on a river; stealing linen, etc. from bleaching grounds; maiming cattle; shooting at a Revenue Officer; pulling down houses, churches, etc.; breaking down a fish-pond where fish may be lost; cutting down trees in an avenue, garden etc. cutting down river or sea banks; cutting hop binds; setting fire to corn or coal mines; taking reward for helping another to conceal stolen goods; returning from transportation; stabbing a person unarmed if he dies in six months; concealing the death of a bastard child; maliciously maiming or disfiguring any person; sending threatening letters; riots by twelve or more, and not dispersing in one hour after proclamation; accessories to felonies deemed capital; stealing woollen clothes from tenter-grounds; stealing from a ship in distress; stealing ore from black lead

mines; stealing horses, cattle or sheep; servants purloining their masters' goods, value 40's; bail, escape, breaking prison, attempting to kill privy councillors, etc.; sacrilege; smuggling by persons armed, etc.; robbery of the mail; turnpikes or bridges destroying.

The main problem was that juries were very reluctant to convict knowing a young child might be sentenced to hang for trivial offences. Out of a total of over 1,000 charged in London, Middlesex and Westminster in the year 1793-94, 567 were acquitted and only 68 sentenced to death. Of those sentenced to transportation or imprisonment, a pardon was often available in time of war provided the condemned man enlisted in the Army or Navy.

Long confinements in prison were rare for offences other than debt before Victorian times. The gaols were mainly used to hold debtors until they could make repayments, or miscreants awaiting another form of punishment. The debtors were likely to serve the longer sentence being known as 'the gentleman of three ins': in debt, in gaol and in danger of being there for life. 'The gentlemen of the three outs' appeared to have an equally difficult life being 'without money, without wit and without manners.'

Those who committed even minor offences were confined until they 'went to foreign parts' or a one-way ticket to Tyburn. Other punishments might include.

BRANDING

This punishment consisted of scoring the offender with a hot iron on the brawn of the thumb. A murderer would be branded with 'M', vagabonds with 'V' and idlers with 'S', for slave. A churchbrawler may have had his ears amputated and been branded with 'F', for fighter of fray-maker. Other offenders might be branded with a 'T'. During the reign of William and Mary the fashion was to brand offenders on the cheek, near the nose.

Branding and the chopping off of ears were very early forms of punishment seemingly approved of by the church, who had their own brand mark SL-seditious libeller,—this time printed on both cheeks. If the offender was one of the wealthier classes he might bribe the executioner so that the iron was cold. Branding was often only part of any punishment, and accompanied the chopping off of hands and burning at the stake. The irons were put away for good in 1799.

41. *Murderers were branded with an 'M' vagabonds a 'V' and idlers an 'S' for slave.*

THE STOCKS

Mainly used against petty offenders such as drunks who could not pay their fines. Sometimes a piece of paper with the offence would be attached to the prisoner's forehead or hat. Abolished in 1821.

A STAND IN THE PILLORY

It was one of the most popular of punishments before 1800, eventually being abolished in 1837. The variety of offences which might lead to a stand in the pillory was boundless; blasphemy, cheating at cards, fortune-telling, blackmail, bestiality, homosexual offences, sexual offences against children etc. etc.

One's fate was in the hands of the poorly-educated and easily incited mob and how they perceived the crime. In 1727 a man named Hitchin, convicted of attempted sodomy, knew he was in for a rough time. He accordingly donned a suit of armour and paid officials to blockade the pillory with carts so nobody could get within throwing distance. The mob were not to be denied their sport. He only survived one half hour of his hour sentence before the crowd got to him, tearing off his armour, breeches and shirt and leaving him for dead. He had been sentenced to a £20 fine and six months imprisonment, but when he heard of the one hour stand at the end of the Strand, must certainly have cursed the judge.

Many offenders barely escaped with their lives; some did not. In 1763 a man was killed in Bow Pillory and another in Southwark through stone-throwing.

Certain offences were guaranteed to bring the wrath of the mob, one of these was bearing false witness in court which led to the death or punishment of innocent people. It was certain their relations would turn up on the day of atonement as they did in 1732. Let's take a look at a contemporary report.

42. *John Waller being pelted to death for perjury in 1732.*

'Last Tuesday (13th) John Waller was brought to the Seven Dyals, in the parish of St. Giles's in the Fields, to stand in the Pillory (for the first time) according to the sentence passed on him the last session, for swearing against several innocent persons of robbing him on the Highway in different counties, by which they were convicted and near being executed. After he had stood upon the Pillory about three minutes, in which time he was most furiously pelted with large stones, pieces of bottles and colliflower stalks, by which he was very much cut in his face and head; then a Chimney Sweeper jumped up to him and pulled him down from the Pillory and tore all his cloaths off leaving only his stockings and shoes on. After that they beat him and kicked him and jumped upon him as he lay on the ground till they killed him. On Wednesday evening the Coroner's inquest sat on the body and brought in their verdict Wilful Murder, with unlawful weapons.'

THE CAT-O'-NINE-TAILS

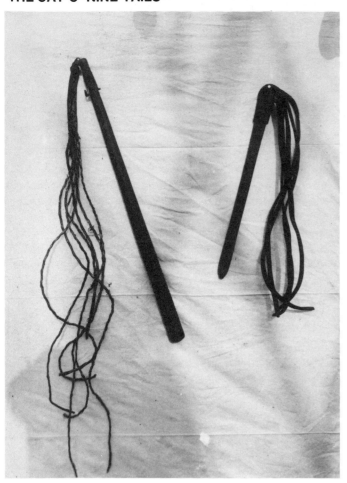

43. The cat-o'-nine-tails.

Corporal punishment lasted a lot longer than either the stocks or pillory and few people over thirty have not had some experience of it during their own school days, even if just as a spectator.

Whipping was a common punishment for petty theft i.e. stealing goods valued at less than one shilling. Specifically mentioned are the offences of nicking cabbages and turnips; robbing orchards and gardens; dog stealing, cutting and taking away wood and trees, and making off with children and their apparel. Other offences which might lead to a taste of the cat included: bigamy, assaulting and cutting or burning clothes, vagrancy, being an unmarried mother or manslaughter.

Offenders would be tied to the side of a cart or whipping post and thrashed with a cat-o'-nine-tails. In Bridewell Prison women would be stripped to the waist and publicly flogged in the presence of an alderman for an offence such as cutting wood in Enfield Chase in 1764.

By the middle of the nineteenth century whipping was used mostly within the confines of prisons and the armed services though by now only on males. Adults, juveniles and vagrants might still be sentenced to a beating, those under sixteen could receive upto 25 strokes and those above, 50. Whipping was not often used against vagrants but might be imposed as a deterrent against such offences as indecent exposure.

At the turn of the century corporal punishment was still a common form of punishment with some 3,400 juveniles flogged in 1900 alone and the practice was not abandoned until after the Second World War.

OTHER PUNISHMENTS

These included pressing, putting heavy weights onto outstretched bodies, and the rack, quite useful if you want to put on a couple of inches. Brothel-keepers and prostitutes might be put into a cart and driven around their local area to embarrass them. This happened to John Bellman of Clerkenwell for the following offence:

'He hath lodged lewde persons in his house . . . lewde wemmen delyverd of chylde in his house.'

The Brank was an iron framework, shaped like a helmet, which fitted on the head so that the mouth was filled by a metal gag, with either a smooth, pointed or cutting edge. If the woman tried to talk she would do serious damage to her tongue. Women would be led through the streets or tied to the whipping post wearing the heavy contraption to deter others from uttering scandalous language.

THE SCAVENGER'S DAUGHTER

An alternative to the rack and popular with gaolers because it could be taken to the cells, was the Scavenger's Daughter, here described by Matthew Tanner in the seventeenth century;

'[It] constricts and binds into a ball. This holds the body in a threefold manner, the lower legs pressed to the thigh, the thighs to the belly, and thus both are locked with two iron cramps whch are pressed by the tormentor his force against each other into a circular form; the body of the victim almost broken by this compression. By the cruel torture, more dreadful and more complete than the rack, by the cruelty of which the whole body is so bent that with some the blood exudes from the tips of the hands and feet, with others the box of the chest being burst, a quantity of blood is expelled from the mouth and nostrils.'

44. One lump or two? (from The London Dungeon).

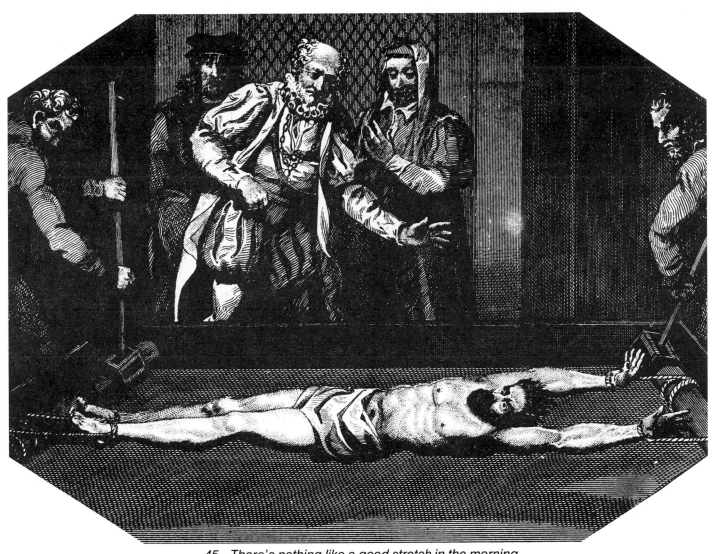

45. *There's nothing like a good stretch in the morning.*

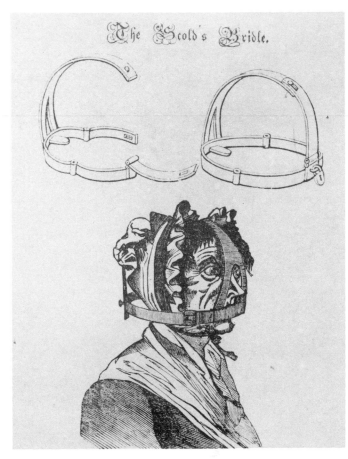

46. *The Scold's Bridle "to curb women's tongues that talk too idle." (very rarely used in London).*

47. *Flogging at the Old Bailey 1826.*

PRISONERS ON REMAND

From the anarchy of the 18th century to the severity of the 19th, the lot of prisoners awaiting trial

48. *Wood Street Compter showing the state of anarchy in eighteenth century gaols.*

Eighteenth century prisons were corrupt, overcrowded and very dirty, with many a young criminal serving his apprenticeship with masters in every crime.

Because of the loss of the American colonies and the refusal by Australia to receive any more convicts new prisons had to be built around the middle of the nineteenth century. The current thinking was that prisoners should have time to reflect upon their crimes and not mix with others, to avoid being corrupted. Thus a silent regime was born with prisoners in their own cells not being allowed to speak with their fellow sufferers and in some gaols having to wear a mask. This second part of the book takes a look at prisons in both centuries, from remand right through to eventual release.

'The prisoner, after his commitment is made out, is handcuffed to a file of perhaps a dozen wretched persons in a similar situation, and marched through the streets, sometimes a considerable distance, followed by a crowd of impudent and insulting boys; the moment he enters prison irons are hammered onto him: then he is cast into the midst of a compound of all that is disgusting and depraved. At night he is locked up in a narrow cell with perhaps half-a-dozen of the worst thieves in London, or as many vagrants, whose rags are alive and in actual motion with vermin; he may find himself in bed, and in bodily contact, between a robber and a murderer; or between a man with a foul disease on one side, and one with an infectious disorder on the other. He may spend his days deprived of free air and wholesome exercise . . . He may be half-starved for want of food and clothing and fuel . . . His trial may be long protracted; he may be imprisoned on suspicion and pine in gaol while his family is starving out of it, without any opportunity of removing that suspicion, and this for a whole year. If acquitted he may be dismissed from gaol without a shilling in his pocket, and without the means of returning home.'

An account from the Quaker, Thomas Fowell Buxton in 1818, showing that conditions for untried prisoners were every bit as bad as for those found guilty.

Without a doubt the most overcrowded prison was the Borough Compter, London's equivalent of the 'Black Hole of Calcutta'. Let's squeeze inside for a quick peep once again with the help of Thomas Buxton in 1817:

'In this space 20 feet long and 6 wide, on eight straw beds with sixteen rugs, and a piece of timber for a bolster, twenty prisoners had slept side by side the preceding night. I maintained that it was physically impossible; but the prisoners explained away the difficulty by saying "they slept edgeways". Amongst these twenty was one in a very deplorable condition; he had been taken from a sick-bed and brought here; he had his mattress to himself, for none would share it; and indeed my senses convinced me that sleeping near him must be sufficiently offensive.

I was struck with the appearance of one man, who seemed much dejected. He had seen better times, and was distressed to be placed in such a situation. He said he had slept next to the wall, and was literally unable to move from the pressure. In the morning the stench and heat were so oppressive that he and everyone else on waking, rushed unclothed, as they must be, into the yard; and the turnkey told me that "the smell on the first opening of the door was enough to turn the stomach of a horse".

The prison was for felons and debtors alike, the former gambling all day long, the latter not even having room for this pastime with thirty-eight men, thirty women and twenty children confined in a yard nineteen feet square.'

The problems of the prison had been raised some thirteen years previously when a man named Nield had written to the Lord Mayor, commenting on the insanitary conditions.

'They have nothing but the dirty boards to sleep upon. No bedding, nor even straw allowed. No fire, even in this cold and damp season. No medical assistance in sickness . . . The room is useless; the floor is earth. Neither mops, brooms or pails are allowed to keep the prison clean. Soap and towels are not afforded to the prisoner; so that a man may, for a debt of one guinea, remain in this wretched place forty days, without once taking off his clothes, or washing his hands and face.'

The notes from the apothecary's book for January 5th are from the same prison.

'Some of the prisoners have contracted the itch. The case of one man struck me much: he was found in a most pitiable state in the streets, and apprehended as a vagrant; he was at first placed with the debtors, but he was so filthy and so covered with vermin, (to use the expression of the turnkey "he was so lousy") that his removal was solicited. I saw him lying on a straw-bed, as I believed at the point of death, without a shirt, inconceivably dirty, so weak as to be almost unable to articulate, and so offensive as to render remaining a minute with him quite intolerable; close by his side, four other untried prisoners had slept the preceding night, inhaling the stench from this mass of putrefecation, hearing his groans, breathing the steam from his corrupted lungs, and covered with myriads of lice from his rags of clothing; of these, his wretched companions, three were subsequently pronounced by the verdict of a jury "not guilty".'

The day after their discharge I found the two who were convicted almost undressed; on asking the reason they said their clothes were under the pump to get rid of the vermin received from the vagrant; his bed had been burnt by order of the jailer; his clothes had been cut off, and the turnkey said, one of his companions had brought him his garter, on which he had counted upwards of forty lice.'

It was illegal for two prisoners to sleep in a cell designed for just one. The governor of the Brixton House of Correction soon found a way around this law, not sleeping two prisoners in a cell, he slept three! The iron rack that served as a bed was not big enough for more than one, the other two having to lie on the floor. Because of a shortage of bedding it was more common to find all three prisoners sleeping on the ground.

In the new prison at Clerkenwell the price of a bed for the night was 6d., although this did not mean you had the bed to yourself. To maximise profits the fee only entitled you to a share of any of the twelve beds available, and, more often than not, you would have to share with some strange bedfellows.

Conditions had not improved a great deal by 1850 when a visitor described his visit to Giltspur Street Compter, where the cells were only half the size of those at Pentonville;

'. . . in this cell, in which there is hardly room for them to lie down, I have seen five persons locked up at four o'clock in the day, to be there confined in darkness, in idleness, to pass all those hours, to do all the offices of nature, not merely in each other's presence, but crushed by the narrowness of their den into a state of filthy contact which brute beasts would have resisted to the last gasp of life! Think of five wretched beings—men with souls and gifted with human reason—condemned, day by day, to pass in this utterly loathsome manner two-thirds of their time!'

Prisoners were at their most nervous just before their trial when surrounded by 'a cluster of ragged witnesses and squalid women with dirty-faced babies at their breasts . . . here and there a black eye or a plastered face and everwhere an aspect of poverty, squalor and drink . . .

A prison inspector's report from 1836 describes the agonizing wait.

'Early in the morning, each day during the session week, all the male prisoners against whom bills of indictment have been found, are mustered in the Master's Side Yard, and before the sitting of the court, are taken down to the Bail Dock, sometimes as many as sixty or seventy together. Here they are often kept day after day, expecting their trials, sometimes from 8 to 9 o'clock in the morning until 11 at night. Some of the prisoners have spoken of this as the time of their greatest suffering; one in particular said, "There we are mixed up with horrid characters, and are like wild beasts in a den. The conversation is gross and horrible; some behave more as if they are going to a fair than to a trial ."

Whatever the outcome of the trial, remand prisoners had been bullied, broken and brutalised by the career convicts.

TRIAL AND CONVICTION
The journey to a place of detention in the Black Maria

The accounts below illustrate two typical trails at the Old Bailey for the year 1730, both for capital offences.

'The jury, before the Court commences, are sworn, one after the other, on the filthy binding of a great leather-cased Bible chained to their box—the leather is black with countless lips. They take their seats and wait the arrival of the judges . . .

The judges entered in their robes . . . , the poor wretch in the dock appeared with a three weeks' beard growing over chin and lips; his long hair which should have been light, even yellow, hung over his shoulders in lank locks, matted, uncombed, in rats'-tails, filthy; his face was ghastly white under the dirt which covered most of it; his lips trembled and his teeth chattered; his eyes were unnaturally bright. His frame—a strong and stalwart frame six feet high and three feet broad—shivered and shook; he caught hold of the spikes in front of him for support.

49. *'Last night among his fellow roughs,*
He jested, quaff'd and swore.'

As for his clothes, they consisted of a shirt, or perhaps it was once a jacket, hanging upon him in rags, and a pair of leather breeches tied with a thong,—nothing else. The man was stricken with an attack of gaol fever, which made him foolish as well as cold; his mind was wandering; he brought into the court with him a most dreadful reek or stench of the place whence he had been taken . . . everyone in turn shivered and shuddered. Some smelt at bottles containing vinegar; some opened the lid of the pomander containing aromatic herbs; some held a lump of camphor in their hands which they kept smelling; some crushed sprigs of rue between their fingers. All recognised that reek and stench for the breath of gaol fever-infectious, mortal.

The rags of the prisoner had been presented to him by the other prisoners; he had no money for garnish, either for turnkeys or prisoners; he was therefore thrust into the very worst part of the prison; he had no money to buy food or drink, so he was compelled to live on what crumbs came to him from the doles and charities of the prison; he had no bed, no blanket, therfore he lay upon the bare floor.

50. *A last glimpse of the outside world from the Black Maria.*

He pleaded "Not Guilty" (to the charge of highway robbery). The trial went on. There was no defence. The prisoner seemed to listen stupidly, holding onto the spikes and sometimes reeling from weakness. There was no counsel for the defence.

The judge put on the black cap. When he came to the words, "That you be hanged by the neck until you are dead—dead—dead"—the turnkey slipped a string over the prisoner's thumb and tightened it, thereby illustrating the meaning of the words, and showing that as he tightened the loop of string over the prisoner's thumb, so should the rope be tightened at Tyburn Tree.'

The prisoner cheated the gallows on this occasion as he 'succumbed to' gaol fever that very night.

Confidence and appearance were as important in the eighteenth century as they are today.

'A strapping vigorous young fellow stepped briskly into the dock. He was charged with shoplifting, an article valued at over 5s., and therefore a capital offence. The jury was unwilling to hang so fine a lad for so small an offence. Therefore, in the teeth of the evidence, they brought in a verdict of "Not Guilty."

The story did not have a happy ending, however, as the prisoner could not pay his prison dues, was reconfined and died of gaol fever.

Once found guilty, prisoners were taken to gaol by Black Maria. One-who-has-endured-it remembers his journey to Coldbath Fields.

'I was conveyed in a prison van; the interior is divided by a passage in the centre, on each side of which are little boxes, each of such a size as to uncomfortably accommodate one occupant . . . the journey was lightened by the conversation of my two opposite neighbours, young thieves and companions in a robbery, who were making the most of their only opportunity to arrange the substitution of each other's names.'

At least this journey was a little safer than one made by prisoners some fifty years earlier, in the report for 1837, it seems prisoners were determined to have a final fling. Describing the vans the report states . . .

'They are 8ft. 4in. long, 4ft. 5in. wide and 5ft. 5½in. high, and will each conveniently accommodate about twenty prisoners; but upwards of thirty are commonly conveyed. No officer, either male or female, is inside the van. It can excite no surprise that, under such circumstances, scenes of gross indecency often occur. We have ourselves been frequently present when the van has reached the prison and seen profligate characters of both sexes, after being thus mingled together, descend from that carriage with clothing not sufficient to cover their nakedness . . . Prisoners in a state of the most beastly drunkenness, infected with the itch, covered with vermin and most obnoxious from their filth and effluvia, the desperate burglar, the unnatural offender, are here crowded together in the smallest possible space; and among them are not infrequently prisoners of decent habits accused of trifling offences, servant girls, refractory apprentices, and others creditably brought up and reputably connected.'

51. *The Black Maria, a familiar sight in the streets of Victorian London.*

THE PRISONS OF LONDON IN 1862

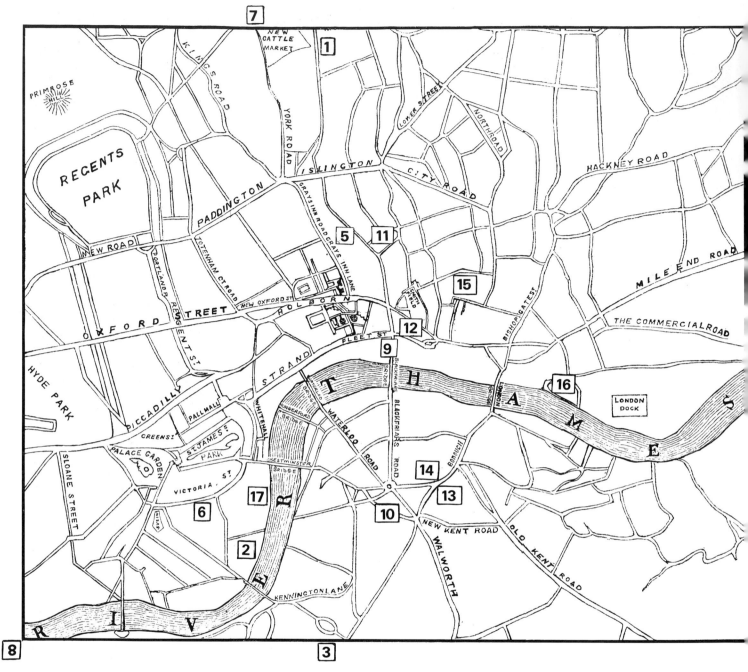

52. Plan of the London Prisons at the time of the famous survey by Mayhew and Binny.

(1) PENTONVILLE.

(2) MILLBANK.

(3) FEMALE CONVICT PRISON, BRIXTON.

(4) HULKS, WOOLWICH.

(5) HOUSE OF CORRECTION.

(6) MIDDLESEX HOUSE OF CORRECTION.

(7) CITY HOUSE OF CORRECTION, HOLLOWAY.

(8) SURREY HOUSE OF CORRECTION.

(9) BRIDEWELL HOSPITAL.

(10) BRIDEWELL HOUSE OF OCCUPATION, ST. GEORGE'S FIELDS.

(11) MIDDLESEX HOUSE OF DETENTION.

(12) NEWGATE.

(13) SURREY COUNTY GAOL.

(14) QUEEN'S BENCH.

(15) WHITECROSS STREET.

(16) THE TOWER.

(17) STRONG ROOM, HOUSE OF COMMONS.

HARD LABOUR, HARD FARE AND A HARD BED

The appalling conditions in Victorian gaols as related by the inmates

53. Reception ward at Millbank. Waiting for inspection by the medical officer.

In 'Five Years Penal Servitude' another anonymous writer, this time writing under the pseudonym One-who-was-there reveals details about the admissions procedure to Millbank Prison.

'I was ordered to go to the end of the passage, where the principal of the receiving ward was standing . . . He ordered me to strip and go into a bath down some steps. I obeyed of course; in a very few minutes he called to me and threw me a towel, telling me to dry myself and come out. This too, I did; and on reaching the top of the step, leading from the bath, found my clothes had disappeared. There stood the principal however, who whisked the towel out of my hand and threw it away, and told me to stand up, naked as I was.
'Turn around.'
'Lift both legs.'
'Lift the right leg.'
'Now the left.'
'Hold up the sole of the foot.'
'Now, the other.'
'Now stoop.'
'Stand up.'
'Open your mouth.'
'Here, take this bundle of clothes, and put them on, but don't finish dressing till the doctor has seen you.'

The object of all this examination is that no prisoner should have a chance of concealing anything about his person. I was then called into the room where the doctor was, and here I saw another chief warder . . . My comb and brushes and toothbrush were set on one side, and my ticket with my name and number placed with them. I begged for the toothbrush.

'If you are particular about your teeth my man,' said the big chief warder; 'use a corner of your towel.'

I was measured in height, in girth of chest, and was weighed.
A card was then given to me with a number on it, which I was told was my number, and to which I was always to answer, as prisoners left their names behind them, and were never addressed by them while in Millbank.
The warder pointed out the way along the passage to a cell, the door of which he opened and introduced me to my lodging under Her Majesty's roof. The little ticket with my number on he took from me, placed it in a rack over the doorway, and shut me in.'

54. *Welcome to Millbank. 'Have a nice stay.'*

FIRST IMPRESSIONS

Numerous books have been written by prison governors, reformers and well-intentioned intellectuals. The most graphic and realistic accounts of prison life probably come from the prisoners themselves. These were often written anonymously, the following extracts from 'Pentonville Prison From Within' were first published at the turn of the century. The author had been sentenced to six months on charges related to a rash infatuation with a charming little actress.

'When the door of my cell snapped to upon me, I found myself in a dark stone box fourteen feet by seven, with a begrimed window-pane, heavily barred up under the ceiling. There was a row of shining utensils for sanitary, eating and other uses . . . The walls were painted yellow up to a certain height, and white-washed above that.

The man in the cell above me began to march up and down. I heard each step he took, clanking through the asphalt and iron-ceilinged roof of my cell, till after half an hour, the monotonous tramp, tramp of this restless prisoner struck a chill into my brain, and I hammered on the ceiling of my cell, to make him stop.

It grew dark about eight o'clock in the evening, and the bell rang at that hour for bedtime.

I then took down from where it stood upright against the wall of my cell, the wooden plank which was the basis of my bed, laid upon it the hard mattress which was rolled up in the corner under the wooden shelf, and took from their appointed place above the mattress the tightly-rolled sheets and blankets and laid them upon the bed.

55. *'I'd like a suit with broad arrows please.'*

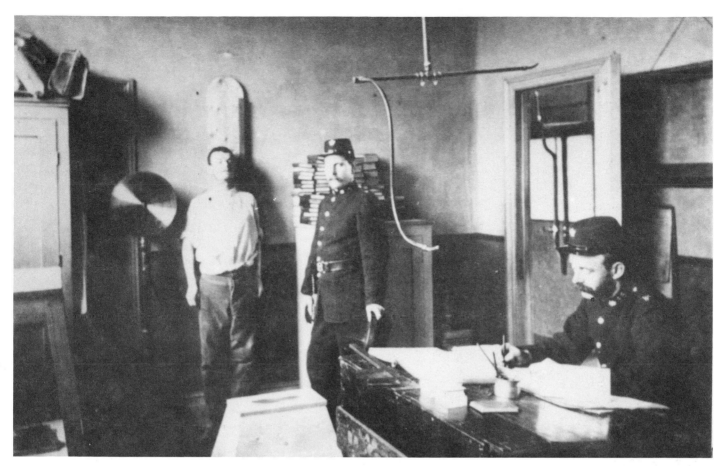

56. *Details of the prisoner's height being noted in the register at Wormwood Scrubs.*

Scarcely had I been in bed a few moments, when a banging of the doors of the thousand cells of the prison startled my overwrought system. This sound grew nearer and nearer, and passed by the critical moment when I thought my own cell had been reached, only to recommence in the far distance and grow louder and nearer once more.

The warderns were collecting the work done in the cells of the prisoners during the day. This work and the tools with which it is done (be they scissors, needle, thread, or what not), must be placed outside the door of his cell by the prisoner before he settles down for his night's rest.

Waking with an oppressive weight of foul air on one's chest, at 5.45 the prison bell, a squeaky concern, which tolls about eighty times, is rung, as herald to a day of hard, unremitting and almost unrecompensed work.

I soon grew thin and pale on the prison diet. For breakfast (about 7.45 a.m.) I was given a pint of tea and a six-ounce bread roll; no butter. I then worked and took an hour's exercise, and at 12 midday a tin containing two potatoes and some beans and fat bacon (a gruesome and nauseating mixture, slimy and apt to cause sickness) and a five-ounce brown roll was thrust into my cell. I then worked at sewing sandbags until five in the evening, when a pint of cocoa and an eight-ounce brown roll (dry bread as before) was thrust into my cell. That was tea and supper combined. I had no more food till 7.45 the next morning.

I soon turned into a pale and trembling mortal as a prisoner in His Majesty's prison. These trembling fits, accompanied by faintness, regularly overtook me about an hour before the next "meal" was due.

Tuesday's dinner consisted of a peculiar, thick, stringy, and doubtful soup, which I devoured ravenously for the first few days.

On Wednesday, dinner consisted of a hideous chunk of putty-like suet. This pudding, with potatoes and dry bread, formed the whole meal, and after a few weeks I gave up the attempt to eat this Wednesday-dinner stuff. I tried it all ways before I finally abandoned it.

Thursday's dinner was the best of the week, and consisted of a piece of steak floating in a couple of inches of gravy at the bottom of its tin. Sometimes this meat was woefully tough; and sometimes it was a mass of gristle. I shall never forget a prisoner in the adjoining cell to mine calling my attention to a handful of clean, dry, whitish-yellow substance, which shone in the palm of his hand like some vegetable matter. I thought he was offering me some extra and unusual food, and grasped the handful from him. Then I learnt, somewhat to my surprise, that this crinkled yellow stuff was the gristle, which he had gnawed dry, of the meat, and which he had been unable to swallow. He wanted me to go to the governor with him, and make a double complaint of gristle.

Friday's dinner consisted of thick and stringy soup once more.

On Saturday reappeared the moist suet, and on that day I dined on bread, water and a potato; for I soon learnt that this brown suet had no liking for the human stomach.

I must mention that a careful examination of the potatoes was always necessary as on tearing them in half, the interior was oftern found to be a mass of foul, black, spongy disease—a great disappointment to a starving man.

No knives were allowed the prisoners. We ate with a shallow wooden spoon, and must therefore tear our tough meat with our teeth. So frequently is suicide attempted, that every precaution is necessary.'

57. *For some, death was more attractive than penal servitude.*

The prisoner was later admitted to the hospital wing.

'But I slept no better at nights, and the reasons for my wakefulness were many. To begin with, I have a horror of vermin, and vermin abounded in the hospital cell.

I woke, on the first night of my tenancy of this new cell to the dismal sound of cockroaches dropping in great haste and hurry from the ceiling, walls, and wooden sideboard, and it was not long before I felt and found one running nimbly across my face, as I lay, only raised a few inches from the boarded floor on my plank bed.'

You grow gradually sensible, as the morning draws on, that you are in the midst of a great cesspool.

If prisoners were forced to use their pots during the night others soon became aware of the fact. 'When an occurrence of this kind happens, which owing to the nature of the food, it does very frequently, the fact is made

known by a nasal telegram, almost over the whole ward, announcing an addition to the already over-tainted atmosphere . . . there was no adequate means of escape for the foul air that collected in the central hall of the prison, and the smell there of a morning was enough to knock you down.'

Just as annoying as the stench invading the cells was the interminable cold.

'the horrible sensation of cold in the morning in those cheerless Pentonville cells. It was not so much the intensity of the cold, for probably the cold was not so intense, as the abominable feeling of always waking cold, and the hopeless and helpless feeling that there was no prospect of going to sleep again, and no possible way of getting warm till the bell rang and you were allowed to get up and put on your clothes.'

Despite its atrocious quality and lack of variety, there was a continual demand for food and very little was wasted. The lengths some men would go to for an extra crust is remembered by Ticket-of-leave-man.

'Owing to my weak state of health I was unable to eat the allowance of bread, and the prisoner who came round to empty the slops, noticing I did not consume it, asked me to give it to him. Knowing that I should be punished if detected for so doing, he even suggested that I should place it in the receptacle [portable w.c.] among the unpleasant accumulations of the day, and that he would take it from there. To such extremity of hunger was the poor fellow driven that he would even have done this to obtain extra food.

I am happy to say that I was able to do as he requested, without adopting the means suggested, by placing the bread in my cell in a piece of brown paper with the dust, which he removed when I was in the needle-room; but this case will show that the man must have been literally craving.'

One-who-has-endured-it took particular exception to the soup:

'In appearance it resembled weak gruel stirred up with a piece of oakum to colour it, while the meat gave the idea of service ere it reached the cells of Newgate.'

Food was distributed by a warder and two prisoners who would carry the baskets of bread and cans of tea and gruel, with only those prisoners with a record of good-conduct being allowed the tea. The warder serves at the door of each cell, the prisoner having his pint-pot filled, then takes his bread and steps back into his cell. A whole ward is served in seven or eight minutes.

An overheard conversation between a prisoner and his visiting sister 'a poor outcast of a woman' shows that some of the poorest sections of the community were even envious of the food rations;

'Why haven't you been here afore to see me?'

'Couldn't.'

'Why not?'

'No tin, had to have a whip round amongst 'em all to get up fourpence to pay my railway fare down here today.'

'Don't believe it.'

'Ah; it's all very well for you to talk. You have your meal regular now. Well I don't. I've had nothing to eat since yesterday morning-you have.' 'You've something to be thankful for—I haven't. Don't you grumble.'

The following account is taken from The Graphic of 1889, part of a study of convict life at Wormwood Scrubs.

'The male prisoners are not allowed to wear beards or moustaches, and there are shaving days on which one prisoner shaves another, and makes him as neat and tidy and presentable as a razor (not always of the finest quality) and soap will allow.

The prisoner is permitted his bath, too—once a fortnight, we believe, is the regulation time—but as a rule he does not regard it as a luxury, and would in most cases be very much obliged if the warders would not bother him with these little attentions. He has not become accustomed to baths in most days of his liberty— ... The baths are side by side—between fifty and sixty of them—and the whole is a well-arranged feature of the prison system at the Scrubs. The water is kept at a temperature of fifty-five degrees, and the general verdict is that it is cold,—stone cold—horribly cold. Sometimes it is at sixty degrees, but it is still objected to, and secretly anathematised.'

'They would like it at ninety,' says the warder in charge; 'that might satisfy them, but I don't know that it would.'

I suppose that some prisoners would prefer their baths more frequently?' we ask.

'Very few of that sort here,' is the reply.

'Might a prisoner have an extra bath if he wished?' We venture to inquire, with an innocence of expression that takes the warder off his guard.

'Do you think we pamper them like that?' is the indignant rejoinder.'

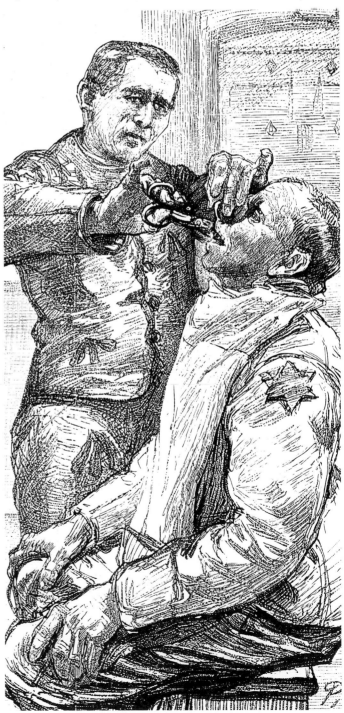

58. *Trimming a fellow prisoners' moustache with blunt scissors.*

"And the true import of the expression 'work'
Is to pretend, to shuffle and to shirk.
Eight hundred men you are; There's work for two,
And if you strive, pray what are we to do?"

The authorities went to great lengths to keep prisoners occupied. Other than oakum-picking the following jobs were experimented with, in various prisons, but few made any profit and there was in general a lack of useful work. Prisoners might be asked to make bags, sacks, ship-fenders, hammocks, baskets, brushes, mats, mops, rugs, boots and shoes. They might also be asked to turn their hand to carpentry, foundry work, grinding, knitting, matting, bookbinding, stone-dressing, quarrying, tailoring, needle-work, tin work, twine spinning, weaving or wood cutting.

Very little of any value was produced and in some cases nothing at all.

59. Prisoner at work in Wormwood Scrubs.

60. Any form of outdoor work was preferable to wasting away in the claustrophobic cells.

60

61. *In the prison kitchen.*

62. *And in the workshop, very little of any use was produced.*

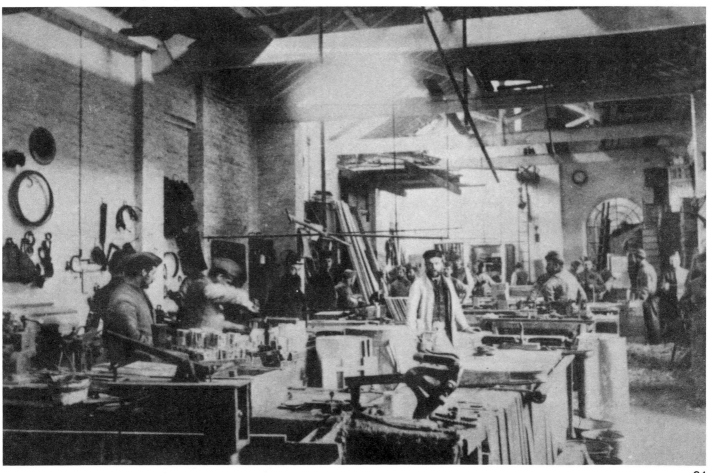

THE PRISON INFIRMARY
The goal of many looking for a few days change of scenery

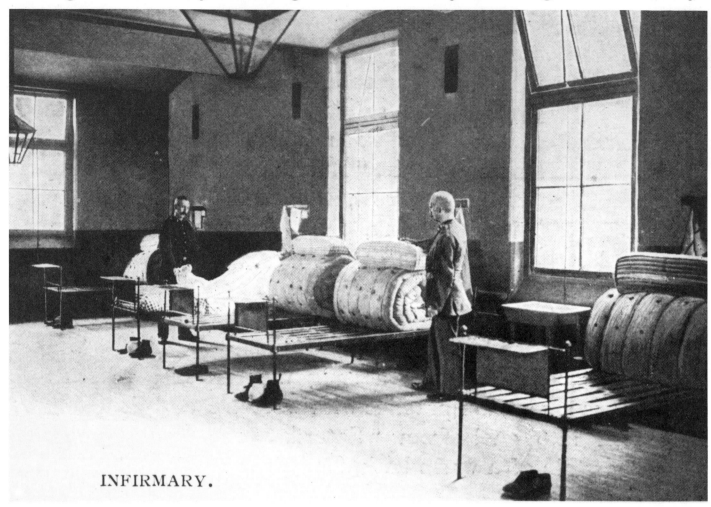

INFIRMARY.

63. The infirmary at Holloway. Prisoners would go to extraordinary lengths to gain admission.

FEIGNING ILLNESS

The lengths some prisoners went to just for a few days break from hard labour or slight improvement in their diet, testify to the unvarying hardship most had to endure. The consumption of soap in one form or another was the most popular way of faking illness. This led, if taken in small quantities, to diahorrea and sickness and if whole bars consumed, to temporary disturbances of the heart rate. Desperate prisoners would resort to eating anything that came to hand to induce sickness, with ground glass and poisonous insects appearing on the menu.

Doctors could not so easily ignore visible signs of disability and for this reason prisoners would deliberately maim themselves. These self-inflicted injuries varied from wounds which the perpetrator would scratch until a really bad sore appeared—to inserting objects like copper wire or needles into the flesh to try and cause poisoning. In gaols outside the capital, where prisoners went out to do manual work, the deliberate sacrifice of limbs, usually by placing hands or legs on rails to be run over, led to a considerable number of amputations every year.

A sort of battle of wills between doctors and fakers developed over the years. If feigned paralysis was suspected, the relevant limbs might be inserted into boiling water or electric shocks employed to find if there was any feeling. Prisoners really needed a strong stomach if they

tried to feign insanity. One of the tests involved the suspect prisoner being given a laxative with his food and an 'ordinary empty dinner tin slipped inside the door' of his cell. He was closely monitored and when the medicine began to work the prisoner realised that the dinner tin was the only utensil in the cell he could use as a temporary toilet. At the next meal the prisoner is served up with the same tin and closely observed.

If he eats the contents, he is believed to be insane. If he does not, he is reported to the director for a flogging for simulating madness.

Most fakers just sought a temporary respite from the harsh conditions, others wanted a more permanent exit. For those who failed in their suicide attempts conditions were rendered even more harsh as a punishment or possibly to deter them from making another attempt! One prisoner in Pentonville 'was cut down in very sad condition, and conveyed as soon as possible across the road to the police court, where he was charged with attempting to commit suicide'. He was let off with a caution but after returning to prison 'was conveyed to a padded cell in the hospital, and there, dressed in a strait-waistcoat, was fain to lie prone on the ground of the cell at meal times, and lick up, as a cat might, the crumbs of bread which were sprinkled about for him, it being impossible for him to use his arms.'

Lewis Abrahams, 'a gloomy ill-tempered man' was being punished for calling the warder a liar. That very same night in the dark cells he hanged himself, the man in the next cell reporting that between one and two in the morning he had heard the noise of somebody kicking against the wall.

Ropes from the cell hammock were one of the aides to suicide most commonly employed in prisons. Those who could write, sometimes left notes. The following was found written in red chalk by the hanging body of a prisoner who could endure no more:

'To Captain Chapman. The last request of an innocent and injured man is that this note may be delivered to a much loved brother.

I can no longer bear my unfortunate situation. Death will be a relief to me, though I fain would have seen you once more; but I was fearful it might heighten your grief. The privations of cold and hunger, I can no longer suffer. I now bid you an eternal farewell. God forgive me for the rash act I am about to commit. The hour is fast approaching when I must leave this troublesome world. Write to my dear sister, but never let her know the truth of my end, and comfort her as well as you can. God forgive me.

Farewell forever,
farewell.'

Many of the prisoners were in a very poor state of health besides those making it into the hospital. Ticket-of-leave-man took particular exception to the prisoner in the next cell to his.

'He was not only a moral but a physical nuisance; the effluvium which was exhaled from his body, and which was to presume, the result of neglected disease, found its way through the chinks of my cell and disgusted me; while the emanations of his mouth were filthy beyond description, and would have created a moral pestilence anywhere.

He said that he had heard through a pal of his who had been recently "lagged" that "his old woman was living with another bloke."

Worried if she would have him back, he said she was a valuable old ". . . . . ." to him, for she was cook at a restaurant in the city, always bringing him enough "junk" and "toke" to fill his carcase, he had all his thievings for liquor.'

Because of the damp conditions and atrocious diet, it is not surprising that convicts (health) suffered. The majority reporting to the prison doctors were genuinely ill though they received little sympathy from the over-worked medical men who had to examine up to 100 in 45 minutes.

After six weeks without a motion, Henry Harcourt was desperate.

'Give me some opening medicine.' he implored of the doctor.

The medic's reply met with the general approval of the prison assistants and officers.

'What a stink there will be when you do have one.'

Haemorrhoids developed but were not considered a serious enough complaint for immediate treatment. The same Henry Harcourt had piles as well as constipation and he described them as 'very large round the orifice.' He continued 'I could not sit nor stand . . . I used to have to lie in this position and raise my leg.'

Most prisoners had literally to suffer in silence.

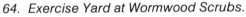

64. Exercise Yard at Wormwood Scrubs.

OFFICERS AND DISCIPLINE
The harsh measures needed to prevent riot and anarchy amongst hardened prisoners with nothing to lose

By the very nature of the people interred, there is no wonder that clashes with authority occurred frequently.

The most common offences were neglect or refusal to work; destruction to clothes or bedding; defacing the walls of cells; talking regardless of the order of silence; occasional swearing; foul language; insolence and wilful disobedience of various orders necessary to be enforced.

A report of 1843 lists a more specific range of offences:

Picking the pocket of a fellow-prisoner at chapel.
Playing at ball.
Playing at blind-man's buff.
Two prisoners indecently exposing their persons to each other.
Striking and ill-using fellow-prisoners.
Gambling.
Dirty and indecent conduct.
Singing and making great disturbance in the wards.

Punishment varied from the stoppage of half a pint of gruel to whipping with the cat-o'-nine- tails. The number of lashes was limited to three dozen, with allowances made according to the age and strength of the offender. In the short-term, hand-cuffs were used to restrain troublesome prisoners, their hands often being fastened behind their backs, almost amounting to a kind of torture, with the prisoner being left to calm down in a dark cell.

The author of 'Pentonville Prison from Within' took a strong disapproval.

'The prisoner who is rash enough to dare question the authority of these boy-warders to bully, is very quickly convinced of his foolhardiness by three days' bread-and-water, close confinement to his cell for that period, the loss of his mattress for a week, and the withdrawal of his library book for a week.

This punishment also applies to the trivial offence of speaking (be it a single word!) to a fellow-prisoner. This is a fearfully cruel rule where a man is in for six or eighteen months and must preserve utter silence during that time.'

When Mayhew and Binny visited Wandsworth in the middle of the nineteenth century, eight prisoners were detained in the punishment cells of the male prison for the following offences;

'For shouting in cell; for exposing their features; for refusing to work, and insolence to officer; for taking a library book out of another prisoner's cell when unlocked for chapel; for spitting on the leaves of his Bible; for idleness at hard-labour machine and talking at exercise. Two females were then in the punishment cells of the female prison, one for eating soap . . . the other 'for disobedience to her officer.'

65. Masks were introduced in some prisons to prevent inmates from recognising each other.

66. *Flogging a garotter at Newgate.*

PUNISHMENT WITHIN PRISON

To avoid the expected resistance to a flogging, prison staff would try to catch the offender off his guard. The following ruse was first revealed in 'The Human Side of Crook and Convict Life.'

' . . . the warder will open the cell door and tell him (the offender) to go into another cell and get undressed ready for the doctor's inspection. . . . .The man who is undergoing his first term of punishment is probably unsuspicious of what is before him, and complies readily.

The doctor tests his throat, lungs and heart, nods, and two burly warders appear as if from nowhere. They seize the astonished miscreant, who is probably too flabbergasted to struggle, and he is frog-marched to a small yard, where the governor, the chief warder, and a triangle are assembled. Then he learns what it is all about.

'*C . . .*', he says, '*you are awarded twelve strokes with the "cat"* and the sentence is immediately given effect.

Each leg is strapped to a bar of the triangle, the hands are cuffed to a rope attached to the apex, and this is pulled taut, till the man's toes just reach the ground. The doctor then stands in front of him, watch in hand, gazing into his eyes. The governor calls the warder who is to administer the punishment, and a big-built man in his shirt-sleeves, bare armed and headed, and carrying a heavy leather thong, approaches the group round the triangle.

'*You are to administer twelve strokes to C . . . . . .*', says the governor.

'*Do your duty!*'

The warder stands about four feet and braces himself up. A hiss, a whistle, and a lash cuts the air. A quick drawn breath from C . . . . . .

'*One!*' counts the doctor.

Slowly a speckled bloody weal appears on C . . . . . .'s shoulder. The thong swings again.

'*Two!*' says the doctor.

The warder is told to stand a little nearer. The lash is swinging round the body to the man's heart—that is dangerous.

'*Three!*'

A suppressed scream—anguished. They nearly always scream at the third.

'*Four!*'

'*Five!*'

'*Six!*'

'*Seven!*'

Only a moan now.

'Eight!'

Silence.

The doctor lifts his hand. The warder catches the thong across his loins and waits unconcernedly for the order to go on.

'Water!' demands the doctor.
A bucket of water is fetched and thrown over the 'punishment man'.
He gasps, flings back his head, and revives. A pause. The doctor nods to the governor, and the governor nods to the warder. Again that snake-like hiss, and the sharp resounding crack!

'Nine!' murmurs the doctor, still looking at his watch! A smacking echo from the wet surface and a long scream.

'Ten!'

It may be enough—the doctor may put up his hand; he may not. He does. The man is taken down, helped back to his cell, and warm water and ointment are given him for his wounds, and bandages if he need them. The ordeal is over.

The flogger is a volunteer, and receives 10s. extra wages for the job. The prisoner lies, half dazed, as best he can, on the hard bed.

67. *Prisoner in Holloway in 1900, dreading the late night visit.*

With more experienced prisoners flogging became a ritual 'pour encourager les autres'.

Courts in Victorian London would often sentence a convict to a whipping to go hand in hand with his custodial sentence. At first these, like executions, were administered in public. Later in the century they took place within the confines of the prison, although fellow prisoners could not see the flogging, very many could hear the cries. At Pentonville this kind of punishment was meted out at the end of the day.

68. *'If you'll just step this way, the doctor would like to see you.'*

'When the door banging is done, night is not silent. They choose this time when all the prisoners have gone to bed, for administering the cat-o'-nine-tails to men who have been sentenced to that punishment. You are awakened by the voice of the doctor calling to a warder, as he stumbles along the dark walls towards the room where the dread chastisement is administered. Then there are the frantic and furious cries of the unhappy victim, and his hellish, dismal howls continue to resound through the otherwise silent patches of the night, long after the operation is finished.'

(Pentonville Prison from Within)

HARD CASES

Despite every form of internal punishment being administered, some hard cases refused to bow to the prison rules and were a positive danger to the prison officers. One such man was a convict returned from Norfolk Island and detained in Pentonville in the 1850's.

'I remember after he had been confined in the refractory cell, he swore, on being let out, that he would murder any man who attempted to come down to him there. He had made a spring at the officer near him, and would assuredly have bitten his nose off had the warder not retreated up the stairs, so that the man was down below all alone, vowing and declaring he would have the life of the first person that tried to get him up. Well, you see, we knew we could master him directly we had him in the corridor; but we couldn't take his life, and he could ours, he was more than a match for us down in the refractory ward. Accordingly the governor had to devise some means by which to get him up stairs without hurting him—and how d'ye think he did it, sir? Why, he got some cayenne pepper and burnt it in a fumigating bellows, and then blew the smoke down into the ward where the fellow was. The man stood it for some time; but, bless you, he was soon glad to surrender, for, as we sent in puff after puff, it set him coughing and sneezing, and rubbing his eyes, and stamping with the pain as the fumes got not only into his throat and up his nose, but under his eyelids, and made them smart, till the tears ran down his cheeks as if he had been a little child. Then immediately afterwards we threw ourselves upon him, and effectually secured him against doing any further harm.'

Many floggings were administered for attacks on warders who had to be permanently on their guard. An assault took place against Walter Miles at Coldbath Fields prison in 1883.

Alfred Simmons entered the dock looking pale and haggard. The thirty-three-year-old porter was charged with maliciously wounding Miles; after being given a drink of water, the prisoner, serving eighteen months with hard labour for burglary and wounding a policeman, listened to the case against him.

The hard labour involved work in a paper cutting-room where prisoners had access to knives. The warder, Miles, stated that he saw Simmons pass a message to another worker behind him. Miles cautioned him that he would report him to the governor for the offence. Nothing more happened that day but the following morning the prisoner approached Miles and asked:

'Are you going to report me to the governor?'

After an affirmative reply, Simmons stabbed the warder with a knife concealed behind his back. The first blow went through Miles' blouse and he felt a slight scratch, but in the melee that followed he was stabbed again, the knife passing right through his tunic. By now some of the other prisoners had joined the affray, pulling Simmons away to his cries of:

'Let me go; I'll murder him!'

The prisoners managed to get the weapon, though not without one of them receiving a serious stab wound on the face. It was as this evidence was being heard that the prisoner interjected.

'It's a got-up case. If I had wanted to have stabbed you, I could have done it. That's an old cut in his tunic.'

The evidence against him was too strong and Simmons was committed for trial in a higher court.

David Sheppard took exception to the public dressing-down he had been given in the exercise yard for not walking with his partner and promptly set about the warder. A speedy and harsh punishment needed to be administered to prevent any recurrence with Sheppard being sentenced to 150 lashes, in the days before the number was restricted. He received 100 before the rest of the prisoners who watched in silence bar two, who uttered both just one word each: the first 'murder' followed by a softer but no less audible, 'shame.'

Isaacs the Jew, alias Fletcher, held a grudge against screws. The stocky, red-haired young man had been a thief from infancy and found fault with everybody and everything. One day he said to the officer at Millbank:

'I'll murder someone, and soon.'

'Well why not me?' replied the officer.

'No, no, you're too big and I've known you too long.'

The conversation was forgotten and weeks passed before a new, fairly easy-going warder, by the name of Hall, was put in charge of Isaacs. As Hall was working at his writing desk he was knocked senseless by a blow from the basin held by a man with murder in his eyes. He continued the brutal, motiveless attack with great savagery and before help could arrive Hall had breathed his last. Isaacs was found guilty but insane and sent to Bedlam, where he was kept in an iron cage for a couple of years.

69. *'If I had wanted to stab you, I could have done it.'*

From the moment of entry, prisoners were treated merely as numbers and not human beings, with no time available for counselling or humane relationships between warder and prisoner. One young inmate, whose wife was suffering from consumption, was summoned to the governor's office:

Chief Warder: *'Ands by your side! Hies to the front!'*

Governor: *'Do you know a Mrs Warner?'*

Prisoner: *'Yes, Sir.'*

Governor: *'Who is she? A relative?'*

Prisoner: *'She is a friend with whom my wife is staying, and she is kindly nurs . . .'*

Governor: *'That will do. There is bad news for you. Your wife is dead.'*

Chief Warder: *'Right about face! March!'*

Warders were also known to drop a quarter inch of tobacco in a prisoner's cell so that another may find it, the offence resulting sometimes in severe punishment. There was a great deal of tobacco in prisons, nearly all introduced by the warders who received 30s. per lb., on occasions, for this prison currency.

Although discipline was greatly tightened in the nineteenth century, many warders still had their price and it seems that one at Pentonville liked his food. Those with friends on the outside in 1873 were allowed to mix with other prisoners, the warder keeping lookout. After the guard had been squared, a prisoner revealed how his life changed:

'The next morning I had the daily papers with my breakfast; the same evening I had my "Pall Mall" with my supper; and they were breakfasts and suppers, for I was supplied with dainties and luxuries which had no place in "bill of fare" of Her Majesty's prison.

At the Christmas of 1873 my friend took him (the warder) a large turkey, a sirloin of beef, puddings, pies &c. which not only fed me, but regaled his family for a fortnight.'

Being heavily outnumbered by the prisoners, warders had to be permanently on their guard. In Millbank in the 1820's, a great deal of discontent could be sensed simmering just below the surface. With the outbreak of gaol fever in 1823, the sick ward became overrun with patients and the noise-deafening. One man who was charged with shouting loudly and using atrocious language denied the charge, maintaining all that he said was:

'God bless the King, my tongue is very much swelled.'

The turnkey replied that it was a pity his tongue was not swelled more; he promptly received a blow on the head with a pint pot, leading to a general fracas.

A more serious disturbance broke out three years later when one prisoner smashed his bedstead and window grating and pushed a stick with a handkerchief on the end through the broken window to gain attention from the outside world. Another emptied a pail of water over the warder's head and destroyed his cell while still more took to rattling their tables. The whole night was spent with prisoners singing, dancing and shouting to each other.

The next morning Stephen Harman secured his cell door and demolished the entire contents of his temporary home; the glass, cell table, stool, shelf, spoon etc.. Others quickly followed his example and were handcuffed before being sent to the dark cells. There were many only too willing to take the place of Stephen & co and with all the punishment cells full, warders could do little to stop the relentless noise and disobedience. Cranks would be turned too fast, bedding ripped up, prisoners incite each other to riot and even dance the double-shuffle! Reinforcements were called in but many sleepless nights were endured by both warders and prisoners alike.

Not only did warders have to control difficult prisoners who were sane, they also had to care for those driven insane by the conditions and not yet sent to an asylum.

How would any of us today have survived the horrors of nineteenth century prisons, with their extremely harsh regimes, atrocious diet and numbing cold, without, in many cases being allowed to endure these hardships with other prisoners? It is in no way surprising that many sought a permanent exit from this world, with maybe the hope of a better one to come. Suicide was looked upon as temporary insanity in Victorian days, unfortunately there was nothing temporary about the state of mind of many prisoners.

PADDED AND DARK CELLS

'Many a night were the whole score of prisoners who slept in cells along that dismal passage below stairs, that constituted part of the hospital, kept awake through the long night by the shouts of prisoners in grievous case, who were confined in the padded cells, and whose brains had broken down under this pernicious system of solitary confinement, and who were now fit for nothing more than to babble their sad coherences to the walls of their cells.

The case I am especially remembering is one of a bank clerk, a man of about forty years I suppose, who kept us awake at night, with a rigmarole about the Prince of Wales and the King, whom he expected as visitors on the morrow.

For three entire nights and days, I say, this man slept not a wink, but continued steadily, and with great perseverance, in the face of much opposition from those he was disturbing, his rambling conversations. Then, at last, he was taken up out of his poisonous cell into the light and air of the big hospital ward. But kindness had been deferred too late, and he was soon certified insane, and he went off to a lunatic asylum.

I should have mentioned in my first chapter dealing with the hospital that we had two men, who had come in as prisoners but who went out as madmen, raving all day and most of the night in their padded cells. There they were, stark naked, their clothes having been taken from them, as a protection against their habits of tearing everything up, including bedding, etc, which they could lay their hands on. Their habits were filthy, and they were found smeared with the most horrible dirt in their own cells. One of them had been in the British army, and was to be heard pacing up and down, crying imaginary military words of command, such as;
'Forward! Right—about—turn!' as he practised his manoeuvres in the narrow precincts of his cell.'

(Pentonville Prison from Within).

Whether prisoners had mental problems before being admitted to gaol or whether these problems developed because of the inhumane regime experienced, is open to conjecture. Prisons were certainly the dumping ground for the flotsam and jetsam of society and in every prison there were some 3–4% who would refuse to keep themselves or their cells clean, or arrange the furniture as the turnkeys dictated and defiantly whistle, shout or sing, whatever the punishment, many being in the early stages of senile dementia.

Others had more serious problems. In Millbank, one prisoner on exercise picked up pebble after pebble and covertly swallowed them, consuming a total of four pounds of stones. Another had a penchant for blankets, tearing them into pieces about six inches square before eating them. Candles and guttapercha pint pots were also considered delicacies by some inmates. Others were convinced that their food had been tampered with. Various complaints included the following: it had been poisoned, flies had been put into it, there was a crumb floating in the milk, there were three spots on the shell of an egg. The man who objected to the egg had probably studied philosophy as he kept asking: 'Why are they there? What is the meaning of it?'

ASSAULT ON A LUNATIC.

70.

Cases of paranoia at Millbank were common, with one prisoner claiming to be deliberately given toothache at every meal. Another contested that a fellow-prisoner, Madame Rachel, was brought to his cell in order to make a plaster cast of his head. The wax had been so hot that it had injured him for life. G would not allow anyone to watch him eat or drink, hiding behind his bed lest an officer put a spell upon his food. L declared that laughing gas was given to him with his cocoa to keep him in good humour.

E.W. was the king of the moon and S had power over the sun, having the ability to make it shine on a wet day. He could always be found at the window waiting for the moon to rise. G.D. would only answer if addressed as the Prince of Wales, although his other jobs included prophet, priest and king.

Other prisoners would change their identity from King of Woking to Colonel of the Madras Fusiliers or have a sister who was Queen of New York. One, not a Tory politician, came up with the novel idea of selling off Millbank by auction. He marked off the lots with a piece of chalk and finished the sale of each plot with the rather apt words: 'Going, going, gone.' (He was talking about the prison.)

Other prisoners invented flying machines that would sail round the moon, or cork ships capable of sinking any fleet. When rejected by the Admirality the prisoner threatened to sell the secrets of his invention to Prince Bismarck.

In some of the stricter prisons where segregation was strictly enforced in the nineteenth century, communication between male and female prisoners was almost impossible. Both the men and women wanted to believe that somebody of the opposite sex cared about them, even if they could never meet, sweet dreams might be induced by some form of communication. As we have seen, prisoners are a wily lot and soon some found a way around the segregation.

Margaret Woods was taken aback as she started to unload the washing sent over from the male block. Lying amongst the dirty linen and shirts was a leaf from a prayer book with a message written to the women's prison for Ann Kinnear to read. It was a greeting from John Davidson, a Glaswegian, who wrote hoping that all the women were well. News of the letter spread through both the male and female wings, and, for lives starved of any whisper of romance a new avenue was opened up; everybody wanted a correspondent of the opposite sex. John Davidson promised to find all the women a sweetheart and he himself sent a love letter to Ann Kinnear, who had read his first communication. As his date for release approached Davidson wrote to Ann informing her that he would get 'a nice young man' to take his place and continue the correspondence.

One day the letters were discovered in the laundry basket and sifted through by prison officials. They were full of urgent questions and answers, gossips, vows of affection and promises to meet outside. Quotes from one letter dropped on the chapel stairs are fairly representative.

'LAST AT CHAPEL'   June 17th
'From the young man that wrote first, to the young woman that wrote last. I myself am not so very particular about having a handsome wife, for many pretty girls are so sensible of their beauty that it makes their manners rather odious; but, so you are a tidy looking girl and industriously inclined, with a good disposition, and will love me, and me only, you may depend upon it. I should gladly accept you and be studious to comfort you all the rest of our lives.

But if there is any young man, at liberty or anywhere else, who is your intended suitor, I beg of you to give one a true answer in reply to this. And I hope, my dear, that neither you, nor your two companions show our notes to anyone; for I know some women can never keep a secret.'

WOMEN IN PRISON
'Women contract the most intimate friendship with each other, or the most deadly hatred'

71. Women sentenced to life imprisonment for killing their own children.

Mr Nihil, the governor of Millbank observed:
'The behaviour of the female pentagon is frightfully disorderly, calling for vigorous and exemplary punishment. Women contract the most intimate friendship with each other, or most deadly hatred.'

The following account is from the middle of the eighteenth century written by a prisoner serving three years for his religious beliefs:

'I observed a great number of dirty young wenches, intermixed with some men; some felons, who had fetters on, sitting on the ground against a wall, sunning and lousing themselves; others lying round asleep; some sleeping or lying with their faces in the men's laps, and some men doing the same by the women. I found on enquiry that these wenches, most of them, were sent hither by the justices, as loose and disorderly persons . . .'

I had not been in the prison more than three days before the Locker, who was also the Hempmaster, made me the following offer. . .

'When sir, says he, you have a mind to have one of these girls you shall fancy to lie with you all night, you may have her;—the custom is to pay for her bed and tip me a shilling.'

I replied that I thanked him for his kind offer, but that I was afraid his girls were all of them troubled with one or other of these distempers, either the Louse, the Itch or the Pox, I added, that some of them, it might be imagined, had a complication of all three distempers'.

The Locker replied:

'I have lain with all the girls I pleased for five years past, and for two years together have not been free of the Pox and was so bad that I thought I should die; but, thank God, I have got my health again purely . . .'

The Locker was once again risking his health a short time after speaking with our morally offended prisoner.

'The two girls laid in a bed in the fines room. The weather was then very hot, and I could not lie in bed, and getting up to breathe at the air-hole, impatiently waiting for the Locker to unlock me, I heard the Locker coming up the Yard;—he opened the door of the Long Gallery, and he, and one of the girls, holding her petticoats in her hand, followed him, and they went to number 3, which has a bed in it, and there they laid together till the time of unlocking, which was a little before six. This debauchery was repeated several succeeding mornings.

It is the intermixture of the men with the women makes this place a scene of debauchery. Every man almost has his particular she, whom he calls his wife, and she in return calls him her husband . . . Neither the men nor the women prisoners make any secret of their amours; and it is so common that the acquaintances (who are not prisoners) of these loose women will come into the Tap, call for the woman they want, treat her with victuals, beer and wine, take the opportunity in the absence of Mrs Jones, desire the Locker to shew them the prison, go up under these pretences, and then and there commit their debaucheries.

Another method the pretended man and wife take is this: the Locker perchance shall unlock the prisoners early; if the man lies in bed, the asssignation is for the woman to sneak upstairs and come to bed to him.

All agree in this general censure, that scarce an hour, much less a day, passes without an instance to gallantry, adultery, whoredom or fornication.'

The prisoner did acknowledge that at least part of this behaviour was because the female prison population had no other means of economic support. Nonetheless he seems truly outraged at some of the language used:

'As for their conversation, it generally, nay, I must say, always turns on the obscene; they hourly, even while they are beating hemp, sing the most lewd songs, men or devils have invented. They can scarce speak a word without swearing, blasting or profaning the sacred name of God. Yet they are great believers, everyone of them implicitly believe all the articles of the Christian Faith; they believe also in Devils, Demons, Spirits, Angels and Saints.

Let's leave our prisoner eavesdropping on the women's conversations. Whether he was tempted to participate in the general 'debauchery' we shall never know, but reading between the lines, his resolution seems to have been sorely tempted.

'They take great delight in sitting in a ring and telling stories of their own adventures;—how many men they had bilked, what sums they had robbed them of, and how many watches they had masoned (giving a worthless IOU) tell how they were first debauched;—how long they had been in keeping;—how many children they had had, and what was become of them . . .'

Prison conditions were to change radically over the next century.

By 1842 the silent regime had been imposed whereby 'even the act of looking up or of turning the head is forbidden, and if repeatedly observed, punished'. There were attempts to segregate prisoners with;
Two yards for felons.
One for women of all classes with children.
Two yards for disorderly prostitutes.
One yard for misdemeanants sentenced to hard labour.

Tread-wheels were continuosly making their useless rounds with the female prisoners 'almost fainting under heat and exhaustion in summer, and, in winter, almost petrified with cold'. For those unable to tread the boards, oakum-picking and laundry work were the order of the day though some of the more fortunate women might have worked in the garden; the silent regime was strictly enforced.

Convicted prisoners would often be escorted through the streets of the capital to their place of internment. It was the custom to stop off for a couple of quick drinks as a final reminder of the outside world, and, in most cases, a reminder of what had contributed to their offence.

72. Holloway kitchen, 1890.

One woman held an emaciated child, no more than two and a half years old in her arms. Passing a gin-house the mother enquired as to whether she could have a last little tipple to comfort her. The officer had no objections and waited at the door for his charge. He eventually had to enter the drinking establishment and saw the child swallowing a glass of gin 'without hesitation or making faces at it.' The child seemed determined not to enter prison as it could not be prevailed upon to take a drop of medicine or the gruel offered. The poor wretch's dying words before drawing its last breaths after a very short life were, 'Gin, gin.'

73. A woman making sacks, Holloway 1890.

At the start of the nineteenth century women entering prison would be searched by male turnkeys. This was ostensibly carried out to prevent concealed spirits being introduced to the cells but in reality was just an excuse for a crude grope which the new internees found both 'gross and disgusting'. This embarrassment and degradation seemed to add to the turnkey's enjoyment of his legal fondling.

'It is a fine treat to a set in the lobbies to thrust their hands about a poor and pretty girl's person, and gloat over her blushes and feeling of shame.'

As in the men's prisons, the silent regime sometimes became too much for the female prisoners and some would flip.

'They tear up and break everything they can lay their hands on. The other day one of the prisoners not only broke all the windows in her cell, but tore all her bed-clothes into ribbons, and pulled open her bed and tossed all the coir in a heap on the floor; and then she wrenched off the gas-jet, and managed to pull down the triangular iron shelf that is fixed into the wall at one corner of the cell.'

Let's rejoin Mayhew and Binny on their visit to Millbank Prison in the middle of the nineteenth century;

'There's one of our punishment cells,' says the dark-eyed matron. The cell was not quite dark; there was a bed in the corner of it.

'What can the women do there?' asked we.

'Do?' cried the matron; *'Why, they can sing and dance, and whistle, and make use, as they do, of the most profane language conceivable.'*
'That's one of the women under punishment who's singing now,' said the matron, as we stood to listen. *'They generally sing. Oh! that's nothing, that's very quiet for them. Their language to the minister is sometimes so horrible that I am obliged to run away with disgust.'*

'Some that we've had,' went on the matron, *'have torn up their beds. They make up songs themselves all about the officers of the prison. Oh! they'll have everyone in their verses—the directors, the governors, and all of us.'* She then repeated the following from one of the prison songs:
—*'If you go to Millbank, and you want to see Miss Cosgrove, you must inquire at the round house;—and they'll add something I can't tell you of.'*

. . . The matron now led us into a double cell, containing an iron bed and tressel. Here the windows were all broken, and many of the sashes shattered as well. This has been done by one of the women with a tin pot, we were informed.

'What is this, Miss Cosgrove?' asked the warder, pointing to a bundle of sticks like firewood in the corner.

'Oh, that's the remains of her table! And if we hadn't come in time, she would have broken up her bedstead as well I dare say.'

. . . Presently we saw, inside one of the cells we passed, a girl in a coarse canvas dress, strapped over her claret-brown convict clothes. This dress was fastened by a belt and straps of the same stuff, and instead of an ordinary buckle, it was held tight by means of a key acting on a screw attached to the back. The girl had been tearing her clothes, and the coarse canvas dress was put on to prevent her repeating the act.

. . . The matron had a canvas dress brought out for our inspection; and while we were examining it a noise of singing was heard once more, whereupon the warder informed us that it proceeded from the lady in the dark cell, who was getting up a key or two higher . . . we were shown the prison strait-waistcoat, which consisted of a canvas jacket, with black leathern sleeves like boots closed at the end, and with straps up the arm.

The canvas dress has sometimes been cut up by the women with a bit of broken glass. Formerly the women used to break the glass window in the penal ward, by taking the bones out of their stays and pushing them through the wires in front.

74. *Female convicts at work during the silent hour in Brixton Prison.*

Our conversation as we stood at the gate, about to take our departure, was broken off by the cries of: '*You're a liar!*' from one of the females in the cell of the neighbouring wards; whereupon the amiable young matron, scarcely staying to wish us good morning, hastened back to the prison.'

75. A desperate prisoner.

Threats of retribution were commonplace in the Victorian prison service, though few were ever put into practice; the menacing words would be similar to those quoted by A Prison Matron in her book 'Women in Prison'.

An aggrieved prisoner is swearing revenge on a hated matron:

'*As soon as I am free I'll do for that cat of destruction. I'll send her first a dead dog with a rope round its neck, made up into a parcel. That'll frighten her. Curse her, I'll give her a bitter pill yet. If it's ten years hence, I'll never forget her. I'll watch her and track her outside; and I have friends of the right sort that'll help me.*'

Matrons might be attacked when breaking up disputes between prisoners. Elizabeth Wheatley was suspected of grassing on a friend's misconduct in chapel. When attacked by a gang of fellow prisoners the chief matron had to intervene, only just saving her life. For her troubles she received a nose-bleed and was taunted with cries:

'*Give it her! Give it her! I'd make a matron of her, if I was out. I'd have her life.*'

Nobody was taking any chances with Mary McCarthy, a note had been forwarded to Newgate stating that she required the greatest attention after several times attempting to strangle herself. Arriving in handcuffs, Mary was constantly supervised but due to her slender wrists she managed to slip out of the bracelets although she made no attempt to take her own life. Because of her 'good' behaviour Mary was not forced to wear the cuffs any longer and started taking sewing lessons from a Mrs West. Suddenly, Mary's mood swung—along with her knife—stabbing her teacher behind the ear in an unprovoked frenzied attack. Another blow and Mrs West's forehead began spurting blood as she stumbled to the cell door. Somehow the door was bolted and the alarm raised but when the cell was stormed Mary was discovered unconscious with a large bruise on her forehead. She did not regain consciousness for 24 hours but this last act confirmed Mary's future. 'Bound with several ligatures by her feet and arms to the bed' she was sent to Bethlehem hospital.

Another prisoner wishing to push the self-destruct button was Ann Williams, a free transfer from Bath with a good reputation as a striker. She needed to be watched very carefully and not allowed: 1) spoons, which she would thrust down her throat 2) stools, which she would use to attack warders, or 3) sheets which she would tear up. Ann was a good header, of the wall, scoring several own goals as she set about trying to demolish the cell with her head.

For her own protection Ann was tied to the bed and a gag, made from strong leather with holes to allow breathing, was applied, helping muffle the foul language aimed at anybody and everybody within the prison. After four days spitting out all the food she was fed, Ann Williams still had the strength to break out from her handcuffs but was restrained by other prisoners who held her down by her hair. Ann went to join Mary at Bedlam.

Eliza Burchall was determined to hang herself. She was also intent on being discovered before any real damage could be done. The young internee persuaded her friend in Brixton to invite the matron along to her cell under some pretence and when she heard their footsteps on the landing Eliza launched herself into space. The footsteps began to fade into the distance as Eliza was hanging by the neck in her cell. The steps did not belong to her friend and the matron. These two arrived three minutes later and were confronted by a body that appeared dead with the limbs rigid, but after intensive care Eliza regained consciousness 43 hours later.

Some women prisoners in their search for attention would feign death but a bucket of cold water brought about a miraculous recovery and usually resulted in a torrent of oaths directed at the thrower. On one occasion when a prisoner was playing possum her friend inserted her sharpened fingernail under the nail of the deceased. She immediately sat up with her fist clenched:

'*Oh, Sal, you are a . . . . . . brute.*'

PRISON FASHION

Not surprisingly women, especially the younger ones, objected strongly to the drab clothes they were forced to wear. Vanity was considered a sin leading to crime and often heads had to be shaved. A prison matron at Millbank wrily observed.

'Women whose hearts have not quailed, perhaps, at the murder of their infants, or the poisoning of their husbands, clasp their hands in horror at this sacrifice of their natural adornment . . . it is one of the most painful tasks of the prison.

One woman will be resigned to her fate. A second will have a shivering fit over it, a third will weep passionately and a fourth will pray to be spared the indignity.'

One 60-year-old, with about the same number of hairs on her head, came up with a novel reason as to why she should not have what remained of her hair cropped. She was an old gaol-bird who had spent most of her life in prison, but was now resisting for the first time;

'No Miss. B. Things have altered a little, Miss. B., since I saw you last, I can assure you. You've no power to touch a hair on my head, mum.'

'How's that?'

'If you please, mum, I'm married!'

'And what's that to do with it?—sit down—you really must sit down.'

'What's that to do with it!' shrieked the old woman, indignantly. 'Why, it's my husband's hair now, and you daren't touch it, according to law. It belongs to my husband, not to me, and you've no right to touch it. Lord bless you, the Queen of England daren't lay a finger on it now!'

The argument was repeated in front of the matron and governor before the inevitable shearing.

Mayhew and Binny encountered the same preoccupation when speaking with the young matron at Millbank.

'Oh, yes, they'd sooner lose their lives than their hair!'

'We do not allow them to send locks of the hair cut off to their sweethearts; locks, however, are generally sent to their children or sister, or mother, or father, and leave is given to them to do as much; they are allowed, too, to have a lock sent in return, and to keep it with their letters.

The locks of hair sent out must be stitched to the letters, so as not to come off in the office.'

To improve their appearance, prisoners would scrape the whitewash from cell walls to use as face-powder and put the ropes from their hammocks around the bottom of the skirts to make them fuller. One woman made a ring from tin foil.

When transportation for female prisoners was abolished in 1852, and women realised they would have to spend their sentence in the harsh conditions of Millbank, pandemonium broke out with prisoners lying on the floor drumming their feet against the cell door causing the entrances to rattle, the whole episode going on for several weeks.

76. Methods of Hair-dressing in Aylesbury Female Convict Prison.

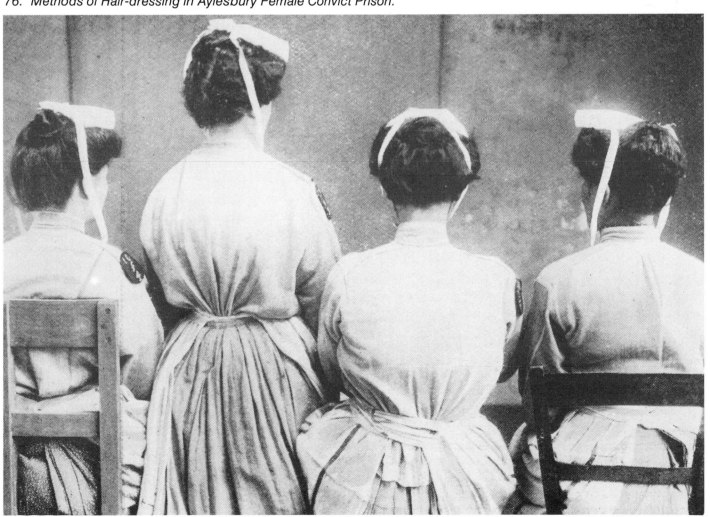

The first creche for prison babies was set up at Holloway with babies born in prison, and those whose mother was convicted before they were three months old, being cared for. When the baby arrived it was weighed and reweighed every week afterwards. The babies slept in cots by their mother's bed in the cell and were taken by them to the morning day-nursery at 8.30 a.m.. Here the wardresses bathed and fed them, and put the babies to bed again. If a mother's conduct had been satisfactory she would be allowed to see her baby at lunch time and sometimes allowed to take it on exercise with her in the yard. The baby was then handed back to a prison nurse, and, if the weather was fine, spent most of the day in a tent in the garden. By 1900, all babies had to leave the prison at nine months.

77. *Mother and child in Wormwood Scrubs.*

By 1895 one thousand women were being admitted to prison nationally every week. Most of them were persistant offenders, two thirds being charged with drink-related offences or prostitution. Most of the sentences were for a period of weeks or a few months.

PRISON PETS

Some relief from the drudgery of prison life might be obtained by training birds or mice. This needed a great deal of patience, though of course there was no shortage of time, and also the sacrifice of a portion of the daily six-ounce ration of bread. One woman in Millbank succeeded in training a mouse to answer her call, the rodent sitting by her side during meals and even attending chapel, taking its pew either in the sleeves of the dress or between the prisoners breasts.

The woman became very attached to the mouse and was a model, well-behaved prisoner. Unfortunately one of the many disadvantages to prison life is that you cannot choose your neighbours. For some reason only known to herself another inmate took great exception to the relationship between her neighbour and the mouse. One day she slipped into her cell and imitated the call the mouse would always respond to. Obedient as ever, now completely tame, the mouse approached its new female friend and promptly had its tail bitten off.

Sparrows could also occasionaly be trained and one named Bobby would hop around a prisoner's table with a paper bonnet on its head. Behind, a paper cart would be harnessed with threads of cotton. Bobby was to go the same way as the unfortunate mouse, singed to death under one of the gas-burners.

VISIT TO A DRUNKEN MOTHER

Prison matrons would supervise visits to women prisoners from their families and observe the pitiful exchanges between husband and wife and mother and daughter. Let's listen in to one of these conversations taken from 'Women in Prison' published in 1863. The mother, now sober, blames her problems on the demon drink, the matron seems to have a rather sceptical view as to what the turn of events will be after the mother is released:

'If it hadn't been for the drink, sir,—oh if it hadn't been for the drink.'

The prisoner, who drink had brought to ruin, stands and looks wistfully across at a pale-faced man in his Sunday's best holding by the hand a little fair-haired child of six or seven years of age. The man is grave and sad, and passes his hand across his eyes, perhaps, as the child cries *'Mother'* And the child's voice—as in these cases always—makes the woman lean her head across the wire-screen, and weep—oh so bitterly!

. . . *'I suppose she can get round to kiss her mother, mam?'* inquires the husband, and the woman, giving a little suppressed scream, clasps her hands and cries;

'Oh! If I only might kiss her!'

The matron murmurs something concerning a breach of rules, and the impossibility of granting her request. . .

'When I get my ticket, James, am I to come home?'

She had made home a curse to this man; she has been a thief, a drunkard—perhaps false to him; but these working men are always hopeful, large-hearted and forgiving.

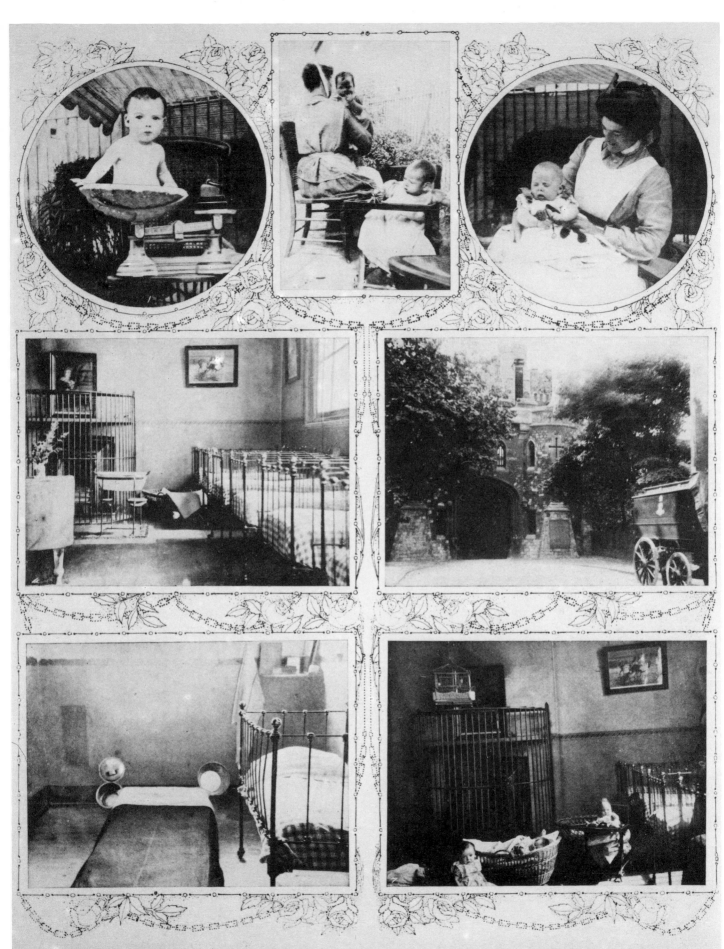

"Holloway Castle" is now used for women prisoners only, and it has to its credit the inauguration of the first crèche for prison babies. In this crèche babies born in prison, and babies who, being under three months, are brought to the prison with their mothers, are cared for. On its arrival each baby is weighed, and it is reweighed every week. It sleeps in a cot in its mother's cell, and is taken by her at 8.30 in the morning to the day-nursery, where the wardress bathe it, give it breakfast, and put it to bed. At lunch time, if the mother's conduct in prison has been satisfactory, she is allowed to see her baby, and perhaps to take it with her during exercise in the prison-yard. After lunch, the baby is handed over to a prison nurse again, and, when the weather is fine, lives in the garden in a special tent for the greater part of the day. At nine months of age the baby must leave the prison.

78. *Babies would sleep in cots by their mothers' bed.*

79. *Sewing Workshop, Wormwood Scrubs.*

80. *Stoning the Donkey.*

THE CHAPEL
Worship in 'upright coffins'

81 and 82. (overleaf) the photographer and the artist record the service at Wormwood Scrubs.

'OUR DAILY BREAD'

The chapel, being one of the few assembly points, was probably the best place for demonstrations. Millbank was particularly despised amongst the capital's prisons and just one year after opening there was a protest in the chapel against the food. The men started hammering on the floor with their kneeling benches, but it was the women who were the main protagonists. After demanding 'an increase of half a pound of bread,' the women decided to go on hunger strike, they having very little to lose having been kept 'half starving'.

The following day they took the bread allowance but they started chanting *Give us our daily bread* and throwing their rations all over the chapel with cries of, '*Better bread!*' The women had to be forcibly removed with the ringleaders being handcuffed.

A later plan to murder the matron, one female officer and the chaplain was discovered and thwarted.

The message doing the rounds in chapel did little to enhance the reputation of the prison school.

'Stab balling Bateman, dam matron too . . . and their favrits too . . . Can't suffer more. Some of us meen to gulp the sakrimint, good blind: they swear they'll burk the matron when they get out and throw her in the river. No justis. Destroy this. No fear. All swer to die; but don't split, be firm, stic to yor othe, and all of ye, stab them all. Watch yor time—stab am to the hart in chaple; gel round them and they can't tell who we mean to stab.'

It appears certain chaplains were not too popular at Millbank:

'Just as the sermon began, a loud scream or huzza was heard among the females . . . the next moment half-a-dozen prayer-books were flung at the chaplain's head in the pulpit.'

Prisoners might sometimes read the evening service. When the name Balaam appeared in the lesson it would be changed to Ba-a-lam, to the obvious amusement of all those present. Bawdy songs might also be sung to the tune of hymns and many refused to join in the Lord's prayer. One prisoner was reported for writing in his pint cup: 'Your order is for me to go to chapel, but mine is that I'll go to Hell first.'

Not many prisoners attended service with a sense of devotion, its main attraction was probably a little light relief from the grinding monotony of prison existence and the chance to mix with others, many of whom were still openly defiant. During a service for women, the call for prayer was answered by a prisoner who probably summed up the feelings of most of those present:

'*Let us pray.*'

'*No. We have had praying enough!*'

Later in the century far stricter conditions were enforced, though many prisoners were unbowed.

'The chapel was arranged in rows of upright coffins (no other word will so well convey an idea of their appearance to the reader) each tier raised some two feet higher than the one in front, like the pit of a theatre, thus allowing the prisoners to see the chaplain, governor and chief warder, who were placed in a sort of gallery facing them, but quite preventing their seeing each other, or indeed looking anywhere but straight to their front.'

'If one looked either to the right or the left or attempted to whisper to another fellow it meant three days' bread and water in close confinement.'

Many chaplains commented favourably about how attentive their congregation was though this was probably more through fear than an interest in the message they were endeavouring to pass on.

'Coming it strong' was the term used for those who sang deliberately loudly on the prison hulks to try and gain remission. Those who sang with such enthusiasm in prisons where silence was the rule may have had an ulterior motive. Brocklehurst describes the modus operandi, already familiar I am sure with many school pupils:

'An intending conversationalist sings the first word of each line lustily and then breaks into a lower tone as he asks or answers questions.' The following rendering of 'Nearer my God to Thee' would be typical:

(Cres.)	'Nearer'	(dim)	'How are you Jack?'
"	"	"	'All right.'
"	'E'en'	"	'When are you going out?'
"	'That'	"	'Monday week, etc., etc.'

One chaplain who worked in six different prisons maintained his sense of humour throughout:

'A man took off his boot in chapel one morning and threw it. It did not touch me but it hit the desk where I was standing, so it was a good shot.'

A typical sermon would be similar to one quoted by 'Half-Timer' in 'Prison Reminiscences':

'You have tried all kinds of ways of the world, the flesh and the Devil, dishonesty, unclen-ness, gross pleasures, over-indulgence in beer and liquors, and you have tried to the utmost of your power the desires of self and your passions. You have tried the crooked life, you have tried pretty nearly every way but the right way that you could think of, but you have never tried God.'

A fair number of religious zealots were confined for their actions in support of their beliefs. Many of these prisoners were morose, arguing points of doctrine for hours, these disputes sometimes resulting in fisticuffs. At other times when God was in communication with them they would hold their heads high in another world and were oblivious to their surroundings. Nothing could shake them from the belief that theirs was the only path and most were contemptuous, feeling themselves superior to everyone else.

83. The Prisoners' Chapel at Newgate, showing the iron rails.

84. Prisoners at Wandsworth were unable to see anybody other than the priest or teacher.

L. H. would spend half his day on his knees at prayer, the other half was spent trying to provoke a fight. H. McK would be found in another corner of the prison, alternately praying and beating his breast, calling on all the saints to save him. H. C. would write prayers for all the prisoners whilst occasionally shouting out, 'Eli!, Eli!'. A fourth prisoner claimed to have keys to the gates of hell: he must have had a good idea already of what to expect.

Many prisoners believed it in their best interests to seem to be reformed characters who had found God and given up their sinful ways. If the rumour went about that the chaplain was on the premises, a Bible would be quickly opened and left on the table, with the prisoner assuming a position of prayer when hearing footsteps on the landing. As soon as the visit was over the prisoners would indulge in obscene conversations through their 'chat-holes'. As might be expected the chaplain had to keep a tight hold on the goblet as he adminstered the wine.

Alcohol had been a factor in the offences committed by many of the prisoners at the service. One man who sang in the church choir and took the sacrament regularly forgot his Christian beliefs when released and went to worship his old god, Bacchus. He only lasted three weeks outside but in that time succeeded in destroying the lives of his wife and youngsters. During his internment his wife had worked her fingers to the bone to provide food for their five children. After his release the father went home and

immediately took anything from the house worth more than sixpence, pawned the goods and drank away the money at one of the local hostelries. When the house had been completely deprived of anything of any value, the former member of the choir rose early one morning and sneaked off with his wife's boots. They were not a pariculary good pair, but without them the breadwinner could not go to work and the family would be forced into the workhouse. The 9d. he received was quickly consumed, and, after twenty-one days drinking, the prisoner found himself back inside, listening, apparently with great attention, to the sermon. He had no intention, however, of changing his ways as he informed everybody that when next released he would spend his discharge gratuity on a quart of beer and a quartern of gin.

ESCAPE

Athough not impossible, escape from London's prisons in the late-Victorian period was fairly rare. Between the opening of Wormwood Scrubs in 1874,—and 1889, a period of fifteen years when over 7,000 convicts were admitted, only one managed to escape. It was the classic flight related in hundreds of stories. After making a hole in one of the upper cells, the prisoner knotted sheets together and dropped the rest of the way into the streets below, making off into the darkened alleys, never to be seen again.

85. A 'gentleman of the three ins'

In March 1882, William Lovett, or convict number DJ 505, as he was to become known was sentenced to a fourteen year stretch at Her Majesty's pleasure. It was intended that the professional burglar would not see the outside world again before his 47th birthday. After previously serving a considerable number of years 'inside', and having been flogged, William immediately began making plans for his escape from Millbank Prison.

As a rule the long-termers were housed in the lower cells, but somehow Lovett was placed in the upper part of the prison. The obvious plan was to break out through the roof and climb down the walls. Being allowed to practice his profession as a stone-mason, Lovett was able to procure some tools and secrete a length of rope he found

86. Over the wall we go . . . .

in the yard. After weeks of patient work, he quietly chipped away at the brickwork near the roof of his cell, replacing the debris with chewed bread. William was a determined man not only did he effect a lot of unpaid overtime in stone-breaking, he also did it on half rations.

Shortly after 6 o'clock one October morning, the warders were doing their routine rounds when they discovered the empty cell. The previous evening Lovett had taken his leave. After getting through the hole and onto the roof, he took off his shirt and tore it into bands, attaching it to the rope he had previously secreted. To make sure he was not quickly re-arrested William covered himself with as much soot as he could get from the chimney, rubbing it well into his prison clothes so that the broad arrow marks would be unrecognisable. He also covered his hands and face to give the impression of a sweep. So, sooted-up, the burglar

began to lower himself down the wall; the rope and shirt not being long enough, the prisoner had to drop approximately thirty feet injuring his hand. Quickly finding some water he rubbed the soot into the broad arrows to obscure them and thus was his disguise complete. So effective was it that he passed several policemen and even two officers outside Scotland Yard.

William made the fatal mistake of returning to Marylebone to his old friends and associates who immediately began making a collection for him so he could flee to France. Then as now the police relied heavily upon informers to gather intelligence and Detective Sergeants Harvey and Pickles soon heard that the wanted man was on their patch. At 9 a.m. the policemen spotted Lovett with two companions and, although outnumbered, made a dash for him. One of the other men was armed with a six-

HOLE IN OF CELL ROOF

THE DISCOVERY

FROM HOLLOWAY GAOL.

THE PRISON ENTRANCE

shooter, though probably because it was daylight the two accomplices took to their heels leaving their friend to grapple with the police. So determined was William Lovett not to return to the bleak, damp cells that he put up a really fierce struggle before the officers could secure him with handcuffs. Such was the force needed to restrain the prisoner that the ever-increasing group of onlookers began to shout 'Shame' at what they perceived to be police brutality.

Thus William was to return to Millbank to spend the best part of his thirties and forties under lock and key.

18-year-old Pickard Smith had fear of no man and no punishment. Despite the seventy-five lashes he had endured in front of the other prisoners, Smith continued to wreck his cell and attack the warders. He spent more time detained in the dark cells than in his allotted place of confinement and would seek confrontation by telling the governor to hold his jaw and the warder to go about his business (though I doubt if he made use of these exact words). One day his cell was found empty.

The governor was impressed stating 'The mode of escape was most ingenious, daring and masterly'. Pickard had gathered together old towels, shirts and handkerchiefs to make into a rope, and, using his great strength, fashioned a hole in the ceiling of his cell with an iron pin. After reaching the roof he made use of the rope ladder to reach the courtyard, later escaping over the boundary wall.

Smith seemed to be about as popular with his 'friends' outside as he was with the warders inside, and was eventually shopped for the £50 reward.

MEETING DISCHARGED PRISONERS AT THE GATES.

87.

RELEASE

When the long-awaited day arrived, those who had been imprisoned for long periods did not receive back their old clothes but a suit of very poor quality often knocked up in the prison workshop and liable to come apart with the first drop of rain. One-who-was-there described his release without showing the emotions he must have felt:

'On my discharge I waited for the governor one hour and a half, standing the whole time and facing the wall. My clothes were so damp that I caught a most violent cold, the effects of which I feel even now. I then was ushered into the governor's presence before the chaplain. He gave me good advice and said: "I hope you won't be ashamed to come and see us when passing by."

'When the prison doors are thrown open, the prisoner stalks abroad, poor, naked, friendless and forlorn, without a penny in his pocket or a roof to shelter his head; his necessities call vehemently for relief, nature must be supported, but his character and credit are so injured, that he can procure no employment: therefore stern necessity drives him, much against his will, to betake himself to illicit practices, and to associate with those whom he rarely foresakes till he finishes his course at Tyburn.'

A fitting end.

We seem to have learnt little over the centuries—the rate of re-offending is still very high. The reasons were all too apparent over two hundred years ago:

"Tis said that from the cagèd bird
Is often heard
A richer strain of melody
Than from the free:
It may be so, but let me sing
My own refrain upon the wing."

Robert J. Clarke. Prison Songs and Poems (1913).

Tragical History Tours Ltd.

PRESENT

TRIP TO MURDER

A unique three hour evening bus trip combining cultural with criminal, history with horror. Jack the Ripper, a haunted house, Greenwich, Tower, two pub stops, live commentary.

MONDAY, TUESDAY, WEDNESDAY, THURSDAY, FRIDAY AND SATURDAY, MEET BUS TEMPLE UNDERGROUND STATION 7.00 p.m.
SUNDAY EMBANKMENT UNDERGROUND (RIVER EXIT) 7.00 p.m.

**Reservations for all trips Tel: (081) 857 1545.
Prices: Adults £12.50; Students £10.50; Children £8.50.
Live expert commentary on all tours.**

Wicked Publications

After having worked in France, Denmark, the United States, Australia, Yorkshire, Derbyshire, London and Nottinghamshire, I recently left teaching Modern Languages to start a new career.

My full-time job now involves researching, writing and collecting photographs for our publications. After being offered a miserly 6% by an established publisher for the first book, I decided to go it alone and have all our publications privately printed which has helped keep costs down.

I believe there is a keen interest in both crime and history and a strong demand for early photographs, detailed illustrations and relevant contemporary accounts.

If you enjoy our books please tell your friends or drop us a line.

Have a 'Wicked' Read.

STEVE JONES, NOTTINGHAM 1992

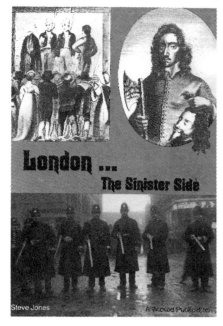

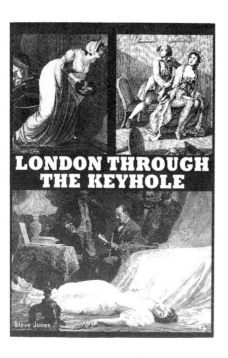

Wicked Publications

Present

(1) London . . . The Sinister Side
Reprinted every year since 1986. Includes chapters on Jack the Ripper, executions, the hangmen of London, ghosts and prisons.

(2) Wicked London
Murder 'Orrible Murder, The Blitz, early operations and the darker side of everyday life.

(3) London Through the Keyhole
Reveals secrets previously guarded behind locked doors. Nineteenth century divorce cases, illicit love affairs, prostitution and night life.

All books are A4 with approximately 80 photographs/illustrations to supplement the wicked tales of yesteryear.

Wicked Publications
222 Highbury Road
Bulwell, Nottingham NG6 9FE
Tel: (0602) 756828
or London (081) 311 3888